MW01200474

People
of
the
Dawn

Jan Fridegård

Gryningsfolket
Volume 2 in the Holme Trilogy
Translated, with a foreword
and notes, by Robert E. Bjork
University of Nebraska Press
Lincoln and London

Originally published
as *Gryningsfolket*
in *Trilogin om*
trälen Holme,
copyright © 1944 by
Aase and Stefan Fridegård
Translation, notes, and
foreword copyright
© 1990 by Robert E. Bjork
Library of Congress
Cataloging-in-Publication Data
Fridegård, Jan, 1897–1968.
[Gryningsfolket. English]
People of the Dawn
Gryningsfolket/
by Jan Fridegård ;
translated, with
a foreword and notes,
by Robert E. Bjork. p. cm. –
(Volume 2 in the Holme trilogy)
(Modern Scandinavian
literature in translation)
Bibliography: p.
ISBN 0-8032-1980-6 (alk. paper)
ISBN 0-8032-6871-8 (pbk.)
I. Bjork, Robert E., 1949– .
II. Title   III. Title: Gryningsfolket.
IV. Series.   V. Series:
Fridegård, Jan, 1897–1968.
Trilogin om trälen Holme.
English ; v. 2.
PT9875.F788G713 1990
839.73'72 – dc20
89-4917 CIP

I am deeply grateful to Steven C. Spronz, Esq.,
without whose timely and generous help
this translation would not have been published.

Robert E. Bjork

Contents

Foreword

People of the Dawn is the second volume in a trilogy of historical novels by the Swedish author Jan Fridegård (1897–1968). Fridegård was born into a poor, working-class family of seven in an area of south-central Sweden rich with Viking artifacts. As a result, he developed a passion for two things: the plight of poor, oppressed working people and the Viking period of Swedish history. The three novels about a ninth-century Viking thrall named Holme and his wife, Ausi, reflect both passions. The first of the novels, *Land of Wooden Gods* (*Trägudars land*, 1940),* chronicles

*Translated and with notes and an afterword by Robert E. Bjork (Lincoln and London: University of Nebraska Press, 1989).

Holme's struggle against his enemies, especially his former chieftain owner, who is eventually killed in battle; his successful attempts to save Ausi and their daughter from death or enslavement; and his establishment of himself as a respected blacksmith in a flourishing trade center. It also begins the story of the clash between paganism and Christianity in Sweden and ends with the threat of renewed incursions of Christian missionaries and foreign trade looming on the horizon. The second volume—*People of the Dawn*—takes up where the first leaves off, continuing the saga of Holme and his struggle against oppression as the threat of Christianization becomes an increasing reality.

**People
of
the
Dawn**

A few years passed peacefully in the settlement after the chief-tain died and Holme and his family were driven away. The chief-tain's wife ruled the aging thralls and her new, spindly-legged hus-band with a heavy hand. A little thrall girl also lived there, and the woman's stiff-necked son tormented or played with her at his whim.

The spring night formed a grayish-blue ring around the crescent of the moon as foreign ships were quietly rowed toward shore and tied up at the dock. A large group of men with foreign appearance stepped ashore, whispering among themselves as they moved up the slope. They spread silently out among the buildings, listening and signaling to each other. Their chieftain tested the solid door, shook his head, and waved for his warriors to gather round him again. After some more whispering, they spread out again around the building.

The thralls who woke up in their hut peered terror-stricken through window cracks, and soon they saw smoke creeping gently up the walls of the hall while dark figures lurked outside the door. After whispering together in perplexity, the thralls decided to run to save themselves.

The warriors heard something, then saw terrified faces in the doors of the thralls' hovel, lit up by the flames catching on the long sloping roof. They caught sight of some old thralls running toward the woods. A couple of invaders gave chase, but the chieftain called them back; they returned laughing quietly in their beards. The old thralls, their gray hair fluttering, disappeared among the trees.

Then there was a shout, and chaos broke loose inside the hall. The bolt was yanked back with a clatter, and people dashed out, choking on smoke, their guards down. The spindly-legged master was holding a sword and blinked in confusion before the grim enemy band. He rushed them blindly with sword raised but was immediately hacked down. He kicked with his skinny legs, and one of the enemies walked up and delivered another sword blow. Then he lay still.

Only three women—two middle-aged and one old—were standing before the thieves now. A young boy and a little girl were behind them coughing and staring with wonder as the flames, reddish yellow in the morning light, angrily licked the walls around them.

The alien chieftain pondered the group for a while, then ordered the younger women and the girl taken to the ships. The old woman wasn't worth anything, and the boy, with his stiff neck and fierce eyes, looked like he hadn't been born of normal parents. They could just as well let him go.

Two laughing men dragged the chieftain's wife down the slope; she struggled and kicked, trying to bite their hands. The thrall woman walked of her own free will and watched her daughter, who walked calmly in front of the group, holding the hand of a gray-bearded warrior.

Those thralls who had escaped to the woods saw the light from the fire grow brighter among the tree trunks and heard the chieftain's wife screaming in shrill despair for her son. The pigs squealed shrilly, too, as the men dragged them to the ships. The neglected old thrall woman soon joined her fellows in the woods and told them what had happened, but the boy was nowhere to be seen.

All the thralls, except Stor and Tan, left when they saw the fire leaping to the other buildings. Someday they might return to survey the damage. Right then, though, it was best to go to the nearest farmstead for protection and to give warning about the invaders; no doubt they would try to harry the whole district.

It was broad daylight when the thieves rowed away. Stor and Tan could hear the mother's voice receding as she screamed for her son, "Svein, Svein!"

The old thralls cautiously approached the burned area, inching their gray-bearded snouts out from behind the trees like trolls. Suddenly, they saw Svein coming from the other side. When he heard his mother's scream from the lake, he stopped and listened but didn't respond. He picked up a long stick and disinterestedly started scratching in the hot ashes, blue smoke still rising from them. The stick caught fire, and he slapped the ashes with it to put it out. He soon found a ring of iron with the stick and laid it in the grass to cool off while he squatted next to it, waiting. Then he rolled it down the slope.

Stor and Tan, mumbling to each other, decided not to approach the boy. He'd only mean trouble. Besides, who knew what might become of him, all alone out there in the woods? They were already talking about how he was the settlement's only surviving owner. Once he was gone, they'd build a little hut for themselves. They could forge tools and weapons and cultivate sections of the fields. The cows were grazing in the forest, and a couple of pigs had escaped the thieves and were rooting on the slope. They'd come home in the evening.

They could still hear a distant scream from the lake. The boy ran and got the iron ring, rolled it down the slope again, then grabbed his stick and retrieved a short sword, burned blue, that lay smoldering before him. Stor and Tan waited to see what he'd do next.

The sun had risen and was shining on the gray ashes and hot blue smoke rising from the center of the fire. The boy looked up, twisted clumsily around, and gradually seemed to realize that he was homeless and alone. He threw down the stick and looked across the lake, but the ships had disappeared behind the peninsula, and his mother's scream was no longer audible.

Suddenly, the boy started howling like a dog as he ran toward the woods. A short distance up the path, he turned around, still howling, and took out the blue sword. He ran past Stor and Tan's hiding place, and they didn't give themselves away. They could hear his howl for a while before it died away among the trees, and then all was quiet. The only sound was the song of the birds in the trees around the burned settlement.

The thralls soon dared to walk around the area, which was still very hot. The pigsty with its sod roof wasn't damaged, and the pigs rooting in the burial grove would probably find their way home.

The spindly-legged master's body was half-burned, but it was still too hot upwind of him for them to approach. His sword, glistening in the sun that shone radiantly above the cove, poked out from under his body. For some reason, the thieves had left that behind.

The old thralls waited all afternoon. Then they salvaged many useful utensils and tools from the ashes—intact pots and pans, knives and hooks they could repair in the smithy. Toward evening, they fixed up the pigsty so they could sleep there temporarily. The three pigs approached distrustfully, grunting and blinking, before being shut in.

The cows came home at dusk. They stopped at the edge of the forest, mooing in bewilderment at the sight of the burned settlement. It took a long time for them to calm down and stand still so the thralls could milk them. All night, they bellowed and pawed at the ashes, but in the morning they stood peacefully chewing their cud on the sunny slope and gradually walked into the woods.

For the first time the thralls noticed that the boat was gone. The thieves had taken it. But Stor and Tan were old anyway and decided they could catch the fish they needed from shore.

They talked about the chieftain's wife for a while. They had served her and both her husbands for a long time, and now she herself was probably some chieftain's thrall far across the lake. It was all very strange, and they couldn't do anything about it. They were only a couple of old thralls and couldn't even offer a sacrifice to the wooden god for her deliverance.

They'd build the new hut among the trees so it couldn't be seen from the lake and entice passing ships to plunder it. They'd live on their own in their old age. If one of her brothers showed up, he couldn't very well object to their having stayed and done what they could for the settlement.

In the burial grove, three level mounds were silhouetted against the water. If the chieftain in the freshest grave were alive, the thieves would have had a different reception. Maybe he could hear his wife's screams as the foreigners dragged her past the mounds.

The thralls pulled a large wooden block, formless and charred, from the ashes. They found the block where the shrine had been, so it had to be the household god. It still had a roughly human shape. They carried it respectfully to a big rock to make it visible from the surrounding area. It might protect and help them, now that it had nothing else to do. People could see the black guardian from far out on the lake, and that might keep them from coming ashore.

They dug a grave on the slope for the spindly-legged chieftain they almost despised now because they had no need to fear him. They buried him unburned with his sword at his side. They had heard that a lot of people do that, and those who had visited distant lands always wanted to lie unburned, with their weapons whole and ready for use.[1]

The skinny-legged warrior didn't have any provisions for his journey either. Only a gray heap of gravel showed where he lay,

1. Fridegård apparently was aware or became aware after the publication in 1940 of *Land of Wooden Gods*, the first volume in the Holme trilogy in which a Viking warrior is buried intact, that some debate existed over the question of Viking burial practices. Although some scholars argue that the dead frequently were interred whole, others argue that in the area described here, cremation was the rule. See Ebbe Schön, *Jan Fridegård och forntiden. En studie i diktverk och källor* (Uppsala: Almqvist & Wiksell, 1973), p. 115.

but later the thralls rolled rocks on top of him—big rocks so he couldn't toss them off and come hunting them.

On the second day, they saw something move at the edge of the forest, then dart anxiously away. They kept watch for hours, finally discovering a terrified old woman who in turn was watching them from behind logs and boulders. It was the oldest thrall woman, and they called for her to come out. After she ate some fish and milk, she told them she hadn't had the strength to follow the others and had been abandoned in the woods. A wolf had stalked her from a distance, and she wouldn't be alive now if he hadn't already eaten. Afraid of being driven off, she praised the old thralls for staying put.

They soon agreed the woman could be of some use. She could tend to the animals and milking while they were busy building. During the long evenings, it might be nice to have another person to reminisce with.

They dug a fire pit in the pigsty and huddled around it during the cold night. Behind the fence, the pigs grunted and peered out at the thralls who were talking about everything that came to mind—the chieftain and his burial mound, his captured wife, Holme and Ausi. The old thralls hoped their enemy was long dead. They still secretly feared seeing his rugged frame and black hair at the edge of the forest. There was no one left to protect them from him now.

But they'd build their little hut so it couldn't be seen from the lake or the road at the edge of the forest. Whoever came would see only ashes of the burned settlement, and perhaps the charred wooden god might scare them off. No one would suspect that anyone still lived here.

After Svein had run howling a while, he started coughing. When he stopped running, he looked around. The forest was quiet; the path wound through the thickets, and he could hear the faint noise of a tiny gray bird climbing up the trunk of a pine tree. From old habit he picked up a pinecone and threw it at the bird, which flew off. Then he was completely alone.

He felt a vague anger at his mother, who wasn't there when he needed her. He still didn't realize she had been dragged away by force. His grandfather was dead, but his uncles were still living at the other farmstead. He'd go there and complain. They had gone by water before, but if he stuck to the path by the shore he should get there.

Svein kept the burned sword in his hand, occasionally hacking the thickets with it. He had a smaller sword of his own, but that was in the hall. If he had grabbed it, maybe he could have hacked one of the invaders to death. But he had run after his mother, his throat and eyes full of smoke.

Svein thought suddenly of all the danger in the woods, and he ran as far as he could. The path was scarcely visible at several points, but a long, narrow, grass-lined pool of clear water showed where feet had been treading for many years.

He happened onto the cows in a glade. They seemed to offer companionship and relief, so he approached one of them. But she glared, snorted, and loped away when he tried to pet her. He had pulled their tails or hit them with a stick too many times for them to be friends with him.

He stayed with the cows for a while anyway, but they ignored him, and he vaguely sensed their animosity. They began grazing and moved into the forest on the other side of the glade. Svein continued dawdling toward his relatives' distant farmstead. Several times he heard the cry of seagulls far to the right of him, and at one place he found the skeleton of a big fish a little way off the path. The shore couldn't be far away.

Twice Svein had to run as fast as he could. The first time, a massive beast, with dangling snout and long legs, was standing to the left among the small pine trees, ogling him. Later, the path had been chopped up by huge, sharp hooves, and there was a lingering, pungent smell of wild boars. Svein thought he heard them snorting in the marsh below and sped off again.

The sun was high overhead when he caught a glimpse of the cove and an islet that seemed familiar. It was near the farmstead. Shortly thereafter, he smelled smoke far in the forest just as he had done when he left the house with smoke still faintly clinging to his clothes. He smelled it again where the forest began thinning out, but didn't give it another thought, just started running, eager to tell his uncles what had happened.

When he reached the edge of the forest, Svein thought in the first surprised moment that he had circled back home again. Huge piles of ashes rose before him, hot blue smoke drifting away from them. The heat waves shimmered against the woods on the other side. He stopped and soon grasped what had happened. He hunched over even more than usual and looked toward the lake, but the thieves had gone. The small boat was there, but the big one had vanished. Fresh green reeds sprouted among the yellow ones from last year. Beyond them, little black water birds were swimming in fits and starts, and a couple of silent crows, turning their heads right and left, sat on the drying poles for the fishing nets.

Svein approached cautiously, then saw several men lying near the ashes. One was badly burned, and his swollen red skin shone through his rags. A round cap with golden wings on it lay at his feet, and Svein grabbed it; the metal band was carved full of signs and figures he couldn't understand.

A horse whinnied shrilly from the forest, and Svein dashed off and crouched behind a rock. From there he cautiously watched a horseman emerge from the forest, then freeze at the sight before him. He galloped forward, leaped off the horse, and approached one of the fallen men. The horse looked indifferently at the ashes, neighed, and ambled off to graze on the tender grass behind the back building.

Svein had feared a new enemy but, recognizing his uncle Geire, rushed happily out of his hiding place. The man spun around, drawing his short sword in defense.

Geire was silent while Svein talked, and then shook his fist toward the lake. He examined the winged cap and determined that the thieves had come from the other side. He'd go after them someday, and when he was through, their farmsteads wouldn't look much different from the way his did now.

The thieves had taken their dead and wounded with them, except for the one who got burned; they couldn't get to him because of the fire. Their bodies had left pools of blood in several places, and Geire counted them with grim satisfaction. There were more pools than there were people from the farmstead. Geire dragged the dead men to one spot, having decided to get help to bury them later. After he had taken the boy to the closest unburned farmstead, he'd come back to guard the bodies from wild animals.

Once the warrior and boy had disappeared into the forest, the farmstead was quiet. The crows hopped closer, flapping their wings, watching the row of silent men. A wolf sat at the edge of the forest sniffing the air and grinning for hours, but didn't dare come closer. A narrow trail of blood led down to the lake, ending in a few drops on some of the round stones protruding from the sun-warmed water by the shore.

The dry white sand on the beach dazzled both men as they waded ashore.[2] No one was in sight, but a boat with high prows fore and aft tossed and rocked near a log landing a few stone throws away. A ridge along the shore rose before them, blocking the land beyond from view. Behind them, the water swelled, endless and dark blue.

The men fell to their knees and thanked their god for saving them from the swords of pirates and the watery depths. As they looked to the heavens, they failed to notice a wild-looking man watching them from behind a bush on the shore, distrustful and half-terrified by their strange words and postures. When the strangers got up and started exploring, the man was careful to keep the bush between himself and the men. After a while, he clambered up the ridge to take a better look, and when they turned around to look at the lake, there he was, an apparition that had sprung up from the ground they had just walked on. Supported by a heavy stick, he was silhouetted against the lake and the heavens, and the breeze caught his flowing beard. The strangers marveled and looked all around again but still found no sign of a

2. Fridegård does not name any of the historical characters in his trilogy, but these two monks are clearly St. Ansgar (801–65) and his companion, Witmar. The date is ca. A.D. 830, the year when Ansgar undertook the first recorded mission to Sweden, and the monks' ship has been captured by pirates off the southwest coast of Sweden, a considerable distance from Birka, the main Viking trading center of the period and the monks' unnamed destination. Fridegård's source for most details concerning events surrounding Ansgar's and his successors' activities is Bishop Rimbert's *Vita Anskarii* (see Schön, *Fridegård och forntiden*, p. 102, and the afterword to *Land of Wooden Gods*). Fridegård's account begins with chapter 10 of Rimbert's. For an English translation of Rimbert's work see *Anskar: Apostle of the North, 801–865*, trans. Charles H. Robinson (London: The Society for the Propagation of the Gospel in Foreign Parts, 1921).

settlement or people, other than the man and the boat.

Before them lay a rolling, limitless flatland, broken here and there by clumps of broad-leaved trees. It was still morning, and fine mists scurried across the land, pursued by the sun.

The men soon came to a road and followed it. They could see dwellings in several directions, and a village lay straight ahead of them—huts with low, green, sloping roofs and smoke rising from holes in the sod. All around were small patches of arable land, but there was no one to be seen. The ground was trampled down near the buildings, and the smell of animals and sun-warmed mire greeted the men. They continued north, and surprised faces watched them through a half-open light opening. Two dogs, discovering them too late, gave chase, barking in disappointment.

The men had no idea how long their road was; no one knew how far north the heathen lands extended. The heathens had built a stone bridge across a marshy area and had stuffed peat down between the stones. Coarse wheel tracks had cut through the peat. A couple of long-legged birds, wading in a pool, leaped chattering into the air and flew rapidly away. Here and there a dog bark penetrated wood and field, or a cow could be heard mooing in the distance; otherwise they heard only the birds and the silence. Around midday, the mist lifted, drifting away in white clouds toward the blue sky.

The Christian strangers wondered how such fierce pirates could come from such a peaceful land. The ground beyond the village swelled into a rise, and the sun warmed the sand in the wheel tracks. Cows walking on a nearby road chewed indifferently and watched the two gray figures as they passed. An old man with a staff in his hand was standing on the far side of the cows by a gray willow tree, but the strangers didn't notice him.

Inside the dense leafy forest, the grass grew in patches, and the foliage shut out almost all the sunshine. Prematurely yellowed leaves fell quietly, sometimes nearby, sometimes at a distance, but they could be seen long afterward, always in the peaceful light between the tree trunks. An animal with huge horns had been watching the men for a long time, but when they approached, it sped away as swift as the wind, its horns cast back. After a while, more light began to filter through the trees, and soon the plain again took command.

Around midday, the men got bread, meat, and water from a silent old woman, who lived alone in a sod hut. When she saw them coming, she put out the bowls, and they thought she probably gave food to anyone who happened by, no questions asked.

The road north soon opened up and became easier to follow; they encountered wagons and horsemen. The farmsteads were bigger, too, and not as far apart. The people they met looked at them with hard, blue eyes, but no one bothered them. At the farmsteads, the children stopped their playing, crowded together, and looked mutely at the strangers.

The two figures on the sunny flatland plodded on toward the north.

The dismal autumn rain poured down over town and lake.[3] Beyond the lake and the rain, you could see the forest on the mainland, a dark, grayish-blue strip. No vessels had left the harbor, and all the sails had been taken in. Only the ferryman occasionally rowed someone to town or to the mainland.

3. Fridegård never mentions the name of this market-town, but it is unmistakably Birka, a major Viking trade center that was established around A.D. 800 and flourished for about two hundred years. Its ruins lie about twenty miles west of present-day Stockholm. Fridegård uses the town as the setting for most of his Holme trilogy.

Holme walked down the empty street, muttering about the rain. A soaked dog tagged along with pleading eyes, careful to stay out of kicking range. A woman in a dirty skirt stepped out of her hut and hastily dumped a pot of hot ashes; they hissed gently as the raindrops fell on them.

A number of white winters and clear blue summers had passed in town since Holme had returned and become master smith in place of his old predecessor, who was sleeping in one of the burial mounds. Holme had built himself a new hut on the outskirts of town and had adorned its door hinges with many-headed dragons and snakes that people frequently stopped to admire.

He passed the hill where the peculiar stranger had once tried to build a temple for his god. The logs were long since gone, but some of the rocks still lay at the bottom of the hill, looking more and more like they had always been there. Holme shook his head when he thought about the stranger. He had been dead and forgotten for a long time, and his bones were probably lying with many others in the field of bones near the big temple. Only Ausi still talked about him; she believed he'd return or send someone in his place, but no one listened to her. She ought to have known that death is a journey from which no one returns.

For the most part, these had been good years for the smiths and craftsmen but bad ones for anyone earning a living by tilling and sowing. The farmers had sacrificed half their livestock in vain for a better harvest, and, enraged at the gods, had armed themselves and sailed out on a raid. Holme had received orders for as many weapons as he could make.

For a moment, his thoughts wandered back into the darkness of the past. He thought of the old settlement and the slope by the lake where he had been a thrall. He wondered what it might look like now, wondered if the chieftain's wife was still there with her spindly-legged husband. Stor and Tan would be old, of course, if they were still alive, gray and hunched from their cowardice and the frequent bending of their backs.

Many times during the past few years, Holme had felt a great need to return. He would approach through the forest like he used to and survey the settlement unobserved. Neither he nor Ausi had forgotten their thralldom, even though their lives were good in every way now. Spring and autumn, winter and summer they talked about that former time, remembering the various chores at the settlement.

Before Holme entered his hut, he looked across the lake toward the mainland. Someday he'd move back; he had never felt at home in town. His black hair had started to show some gray, his daughter was half-grown, and he could afford to build a house anywhere he wanted. Wherever he went, he could have a smithy. Ausi talked now and then about how she wanted someday to have a plot of land and a few animals.

As Holme stood there gazing toward the mainland, the three-day rain stopped and a brassy yellow stripe of sky rose slowly from the earth in the west. The sun broke through a crack in the clouds for a moment, casting its brilliant evening light on soaking wet log walls and green sod roofs. The rainwater ran a moment longer, trickling in rivulets along the rocky streets.[4]

After the sun had passed the narrow crack, Holme walked into the forest; dusk fell. Holme listened to the sounds—the gentle rippling of water, the barking of dogs, the yells and noises from the

4. Stone paving would have been unusual during this period, as an observation in the Old English poem *Beowulf* suggests: "The road was decorated with stones" (line 320). Such an observation would not have occurred had stone paving been normal. Archeologists think that the streets of Birka were paved with wood. See Bertil Almgren, ed., *The Viking* (London: C. A. Watts, 1966), p. 39.

harbor. On the distant mainland, someone lit a fire that sputtered reluctantly, then finally burned strong. Holme shook his head at the memories from that place and walked into his hut.

Two homeless people, Svein and his uncle Geire, came through the woods on the path connecting the two burned farmsteads. They had just passed Geire's and had seen the piles of ashes. A summer's wind and rain had compacted them, making assorted objects stick out—here a hinge, there the black legs of a tripod. The path to the lake was harder to see than before, and the log landing, whitened by sun and rain, had collapsed on one side.

Geire walked with a gloomy face, and Svein plodded along silently. The rain gradually stopped, and the evening sun shone between the tree trunks. For a moment, everything was lit up in the yellowish-green glow after the rain—stones, tall ferns, blades of grass, and the branches on the ground. In the open areas, sparse swarms of large autumn mosquitos still danced in the last rays of sunlight.

Once the sun had gone down, the woods quickly grew dark, and a raw chill rose from the hollows. The bow hanging on Geire's back creaked with every step he took. Svein constantly looked to the sides, turning his whole upper body. Several times, he thought he saw trolls lurking in the darkness. He thrust his sword at them, and they came no closer. The winged cap, with the unfamiliar insignia, hung on a thong over his shoulder.

In the last of the dusk, they recognized the lookout hill and the slope running from it to the settlement. Cowpaths were visible here and there in the thickets, which Geire was surprised to see freshly trampled—the smell of cattle filled the air. They hadn't seen any animals at his farmstead; the raiders had undoubtedly stolen them.

"Were the cows here when it burned, Svein?"

"No, in the woods."

So they were still there. They caught a glimpse of them among the trees. But who had milked them and why were they still going home to the burned settlement? Maybe some outlaw had taken refuge there. There might be trolls, too, or some other forest creatures now that no humans were around to keep them at bay.

They walked around the piles of ashes but saw nothing unusual. The pigsty was still there in the darkness, but they didn't think of entering it. They made a bed of spruce twigs on the damp ground close to the cows. Geire took some meat and bread out of his birch-bark box. While they ate, it occurred to him that he could get a little milk for the wooden tankard they had with them. The cows belonged to him and the boy, but they couldn't take them along. Maybe they'd find a farmstead where they could sell or barter them for a couple of horses and better equipment. His sister and her skinny-legged husband had kept no horses the last few years.

One cow stood chewing indifferently and let Geire milk her. She showed signs of already having been milked that evening, and again he thought about trolls and highwaymen. Where were they now? Had they hidden, waiting for him and the boy to leave? He had better keep an eye open; an arrow or a spear might come flying silently through the darkness.

The ground was damp under the twigs, but they sat down anyway, their legs heavy after the day's journey. Svein lay down on his side and was soon asleep, but Geire didn't dare lie down. The out-law might not have a bow or a spear, but he could sneak up on a sleeping man with an ax, a stick, or a rock. Geire kept diligent watch, and many strange noises came from the dark and silent night.

He would rather have moved on before nightfall, but Svein needed to sleep. The boy was a hindrance, but they were the only two family survivors; they had much to avenge. He was a peculiar boy, sulky and strong like his father, but with his mother's blond hair and plain features. And his stiff neck, the legacy of the smith's stone, might not be as noticeable once he was grown and had long hair and a beard.

Svein's mother was probably a thrall now for some chieftain in the east. If Geire heard of someone going that way on a raid, he would join him. The gods would surely help him ferret out the invaders. He was a single man and had no desire to rebuild the farmstead. He would spend the rest of his life offering his arm and sword to some marauding chieftain.

Geire's thoughts were interrupted by something like a door thudding shut, followed by distinct grunting. You could hear such things in the night where people had once lived for a long time. Somebody probably hadn't been properly buried. In any case, he ought to move on with the boy; it was no good staying there. Just then, he thought he heard the ashes mumbling. His beard stood on end and chills ran up and down his spine. He reached out to wake the boy but hesitated. Svein was sleeping so soundly, his face white and fatigued in the soft glow of the moon.

A moment later, he saw something moving on the slope. The creature was all hunched over, its hair a radiant white under a kerchief. It was neither man nor woman and looked most like a gray rag floating fitfully along, stopping intermittently. Geire mumbled something and placed his sword between himself and the ghost, which glided toward the ashes and disappeared in front of them. A cow standing higher up the slope turned its head and gave out a prolonged moo, and the sound of splashing waves suddenly roared loudly across the slope as if the shore were getting nearer. Then everything fell quiet again.

Geire didn't dare wait for what might happen next. He shook Svein's arm, and the boy sat up peevishly. They didn't say a word; Geire got up and started walking with Svein following him as before. They didn't know that two relieved old thralls watched them from behind the pigsty. Against the hazy sky in the west, Stor and Tan saw the stately man and the stiff-necked boy silhouetted for a moment before they disappeared down the forest path.

A few mornings later, the thralls awoke to a noise and cows mooing. They peered cautiously out, suspecting wolves or bears, but instead saw strangers catching the cows. The ones they couldn't catch they drove into the forest. The thralls watched bitterly but didn't dare show themselves. They knew this was the result of Geire's visit. It wouldn't be easy to get by without cows once winter came.

A few days' journey to the south, two gray-clad men were wandering north. They had walked for several days after the pirates had put them ashore. Many times, death—in the form of outlaws and half-wild heathens—had peered at them from the forest. Perhaps their impoverished look saved them. Other times they had slept peacefully under the roofs and eaten the food of friendly heathens. They passed graveyards filled with numberless burial mounds and, a couple of times, containing tall gray stones bearing mysterious symbols. The land seemed endless, and the leafy woods had given way to an expansive dark pine forest. An icy wind blew from the clear blue horizon in front of them, and all day frost clung to the north side of the lingonberry tufts.

The men plodded on without rest, hoping to reach their destination before the heathen land's hard white winter set in.

Ausi and the other women waiting in the harbor saw the milk boat approaching at a distance from the mainland. Every morning they carried their wooden tankards down to fill them with milk still warm from the udder. There weren't many cattle on the island, and they couldn't supply the whole town.

The autumn morning was cool and gray before the sun came up, and the icy water lapped the dock's wooden pilings. As the boat came closer Ausi could see its foaming wooden prow, the oarsman, and two identical figures. People came across with the milk boat every day, but something about these two made Ausi stare and gave her a strange feeling. Her heart began pounding when one said a few words as he handed the oarsman something. The foreign sound and gentleness of the voice called the sacrificial stranger back from the darkness of the years enveloping him. Ausi could see him standing in the clear blue water again, smiling, offering her his hand that day of the summer baptism. She remembered his cross reflecting in the water below her bowed head. The two new strangers were walking across the gangway now, and she caught the first one's eye. He had the stranger's gaze—gentle, unfathomable.

The sun rose over the town's sod roofs glaring yellow-green in the first rays of light. As if in a vivid dream, Ausi saw a cross flash on the new stranger's chest as he stepped down from the gangway. It was the cross from the past. Without thinking, she started following him, until the oarsman's laughing voice caught up with her, asking if she planned on going home with an empty tankard. The sight of the wind rustling a clump of reeds brought Ausi to her senses, and she turned around.

The oarsman knew that the men were Christians from a faraway land. The king had sent for them, and they were men of high station, even though they had come by foot. The oarsman asked the women if they remembered the stranger who had tried to build a church on the hill. But Ausi didn't answer and didn't hear the oarsman's comment that you could live as a Christian only with the king's permission.

She was still watching the two figures walking west along the shore toward the fortress. Neither was the sacrificed priest, but he had to have sent them. The stranger had said that he or someone else would come until all the people had cast off their wooden gods and turned to Christ, the One who could and would call the dead back from the grave.

Ausi was filled with anxiety and happiness all the way home. The hunger in her heart, which she remembered from when the stranger was there, had returned. She didn't know how she could stand waiting until she heard more about the new strangers. Maybe they knew a little about her, that she had been baptized. The look one of them had given her was full of something like love, but was nothing like what the men in town expressed when they ogled her now and then. She knew perfectly well what they wanted.

Maybe the strangers could perceive that Ausi had had the water poured on her head once—that she belonged to those who would not die and be gone forever.

The thought bloomed inside her like a radiant, beautiful meadow, but a black shadow soon fell in the midst of it: Holme. He loathed the Christians, and his look darkened whenever she talked of them. And Tora, their daughter, was just like her father. Holme never traded with Christian merchants and had once laughed derisively at Christ, saying he was a lesser man than the wooden gods—pale and feeble as a woman—whose followers refused to fight, had timid eyes, and cried easily. Holme knew many Christians in town even though they had no priest. He, on the other hand, had always managed without either the wooden gods or Christ.

As far as Ausi knew she was the only one left who had been baptized back then. The old warrior now slept in one of the green mounds outside town; the younger one had sailed off to a distant land and had not returned with the ship. She hadn't seen the women for a long time—they probably weren't in town any more. If the new strangers didn't look for her, she would go and tell them about her baptism. But Holme would be enraged again, and the peace of the last few years would be gone.

Ausi was afraid to go back to Holme and Tora with her heart full of such joy. Both had piercing, dark eyes, and it wasn't easy to hide anything from them. They had already opened the light openings, so it had to be fully lighted inside, and Holme would see from her face that something had happened. She didn't want to tell him about the strangers, not yet. He'd remember everything from the past, and that could jeopardize their lives. Back then, Holme had been a runaway thrall but still dangerous; what couldn't he do now that he was a respected man? Many would stand at his side against the Christian strangers. Christ was powerful, but who could stand up against Holme?

She saw the men once more before she reached her house. The two figures in the distance were walking slowly up the slope toward the fortress. The wind had turned cold, and snow was starting to fall from the blue sky. The mainland was scarcely visible through the veil of flakes. Snow usually didn't fall from a clear sky; this might be a sign from Christ that his men had reached their destination. Or it might even be a warning from the wooden gods. The men stood at the gate as if hesitating to go in, after all. But then maybe the guard had stopped them.

The snow fell harder, and soon Ausi could see only those buildings closest to her. The soot piles, the garbage, and the roofs soon glittered white, and when she looked up, the blue sky had vanished in a gray-white chaos of flakes. She could tell Holme about the strange snowfall, and he wouldn't notice anything unusual in her face.

Holme was sitting on his bench deep in thought when Ausi came in with the milk, and Tora was asleep, her black hair encircling her face. Finally Holme spoke a few words about his dream of the mainland, but Ausi felt resistant again. She didn't want to leave town now—not before she had received a message from the one coming to life again in her heart.

After breakfast, Holme walked to the smithy at the edge of town. He was often in a bad mood in the morning and didn't want to talk to anyone. The pigs were grubbing in the road, and one that didn't get out of the way got a kick that sent it flying.

His helpers, already waiting outside, started talking with their quiet master. A couple of them had been there in the old days when they tore down the stranger's partially built church; the others were thralls Holme had bought and set free. Holme, never forgetting his own days as a thrall, divided the smithy earnings equally among those who worked there, much to the surprise of anyone hearing about it, and much to Ausi's anger. Holme had thralls and craftsmen for friends, although merchants and chieftains both sought him out and would have liked to have him as their guest.

The smiths opened the windows, and a ray of light shot into the smithy, which smelled of soot and iron. Completed weapons were hanging on the walls; half-finished and newly begun weapons lay in rows by the hearth. Anvils sat on the sooty, earthen floor, fastened to heavy oak stumps. Stone molds were strewn on a bench.

There were other smithies nearby; the clang of sledgehammers and the song of the smiths could be heard throughout town, if no other noises drowned them out. Other craftsmen had their huts and sheds close to the smithies. Some made combs, boxes, and other things out of horn or bone; others were silversmiths and potters. Craftsmen from everywhere flocked together, as windows and doors were opened to the new day.

Many kinds of people visited the town to buy or barter for various goods. Farmers came from the mainland with grain and meat; beautifully and expensively dressed merchants came from the foreign ships with ornamented earthenware more beautiful than that made in town, gold-laced ribbons and silk fabrics, glass bowls and pearls. Warriors came to Holme, wanting new edges on their swords, spears, or arrow tips, and farmers came, needing points for their plows or wanting other tools and fittings.

It was still morning when Holme and the smiths saw two figures standing in the door, an older warrior and a boy. The two blinked at the darkness for a moment before coming in, and the vague memory their presence awoke in Holme puzzled him. The boy had a short sword that had been in a fire, and the warrior asked if Holme could repair it. Or would it be better to buy the boy another sword?

His blue eyes opened wide, the boy watched the dark figure of the smith the whole time. He recognized Holme from his mother's description and his own nightmares. As long as he could remember, his mother had warned him that if he ventured into the forest alone, a dark man would come and hurt him. She had frequently described him, and he was the man in charge of the smithy.

Geire looked pensively at Holme, but couldn't remember

where he had seen him before. Perhaps from some bartering when his brothers were alive.

Holme recognized the burned sword as soon as he took hold of it. He had forged it at the cleft in the rocks when he was still a thrall. It was the first time in many years that he had held any of his old work, and he examined it closely without saying anything. He caught a glimpse of the boy's eyes, filled with wonder and terror, and he felt some bitter memory move in his depths.

Holme said nothing, merely offered the warrior a new sword in exchange for the burned one. Geire accepted his offer in surprise, and the terror in Svein's eyes disappeared behind his happiness over the new sword. The smiths laughed and watched his strange movements. He turned his whole body where he wanted to look. On the thong over his shoulder, he still carried the alien winged cap.

After they left, Holme walked to the door and watched them, still scouring his memory, marveling over what they had brought to life. At the same time, Svein turned his upper body and looked back; instantly everything became clear to Holme. He gave a start as if to follow them, and Svein clutched Geire in terror. Soon they turned a corner and were gone. All day long, Holme kept thinking about the time he had fled with Ausi and their baby, and he remembered the day at the edge of the forest when, with a stone, he had marked the chieftain's son forever.

Something must have happened at the old settlement. He'd go back there again someday and see it all again—the cleft in the rocks, his old smithy; the dogs, if they were still alive, that were his friends; and the cave in the forest, their former home. He didn't care about the people.

He noticed that the streets were pretty lively, the way they alays were when the king was in town. Just as Holme started to go back into the smithy, two strange figures walked by on the opposite street, two men neither warriors, merchants, nor craftsmen. They were more dangerous than most though they didn't often carry weapons. There could be no doubt what their mission was if you remembered the one who had once wanted to build a church, the one who finally hung, eyes shut, in the tree outside the huge temple housing the wooden gods.

When Holme went inside, the smiths could tell something was wrong, but they knew nothing yet about the two Christians who had arrived that morning.

By the time the ground was bare again, there were many Christians in town who had already raised a small church by the courtyard outside the chieftain's quarters. Across the yard, one of the heathens had donated space for a shrine to house a lofty wooden god. Twice as tall as a man, it stood looking grimly toward the church. Neither god seemed able to drive the other away; both stood fast although the shrine's sacrificial smoke occasionally encircled the church, and the smell of burning flesh forced its way to the Christian altar. And the wooden god's servant, who had lit the fire, could hear songs and calls to Christ rising from the glistening gold and silver church.

An open area separated the shrine and the church, perhaps intended by the heathens as a place for the gods to fight. One day, after sacrificing fruitlessly to the wooden god, an enraged heathen walked insolently across to see if Christ had more power to help. Once they saw that the wooden god was unmoved and that nothing bad had befallen the blasphemer, several others followed. One of the strangers in the Christian church received them joyfully and promised that Christ would soon help them out of all their difficulties and troubles. They stood apprehensively in front of His altar, stealing occasional furtive glances through the door where they could see the gigantic, grayish-red wooden god searching for them with rigid, menacing eyes.

At the autumn assembly, the foreign monks obtained permission to preach wherever and whenever they wanted. Immediately, they began marching around, fearlessly talking about their god's remarkable qualities. Holme saw them frequently, and once they came into the smithy. One started to talk, already having learned enough of the Norse tongue to be understood. Holme's face was hard as wood, and he walked toward them, sledgehammer raised. They cowered out of the dark figure's way, and the one in front said his time had not yet come.

When they were outside, Holme told them in his gruff voice that they wouldn't have any better luck than their fellow countryman had many years before, but they just looked at him in surprise and didn't respond. Maybe they didn't know about their countryman. Behind Holme, his smiths watched, laughing scornfully. Curious, derisive faces peered out from the other smithies and craftsmen's sheds, and the strangers felt death closing in on them. They left the craftsmen's quarter where the work would be hard and dangerous and walked back toward town again.

Rumors about their work soon started making the rounds. The town's chieftain, who was the most powerful man next to the king, had joined them, and the Christians lived securely in his court and held their meetings there.[5] Many attended them to gain favor with the chieftain, and others attended out of curiosity. Numerous

5. This chieftain is likely modeled after the chieftain named Herigar described by Rimbert. See *Anskar,* chapter 11, p. 49.

merchants freed the thralls they had captured in Christian lands.

All the while, Ausi floated around in uneasy excitement, and Holme looked at her now and then with a stern warning in his eye. The past had returned, and she felt often that the Christian stranger's teaching, filled with peace, had brought her only strife and unpleasantness. Still she couldn't stop thinking about everything the new god had promised His followers, and besides she was still bound to Him because of her baptism. She wished that Christ would tell the new strangers about it. Holme would never allow her to approach them.

But a rumor about the wooden gods had sprung up too, making it clear that they had no intention of letting Christ come to power. In a private shrine the battle god had stretched forth his arm toward the Christian buildings and yard during a sacrifice. Both the warrior who owned the shrine and the people who lived in his house had seen it, and now the heathens were eagerly waiting to see what would happen to the Christians. Others had noticed countless sails gradually changing into clouds on the horizon. That had to portend impending evil.

Although it was late in the year and the days were short, no snow fell and the lakes had not frozen over. One day, a light blazed across the half-dark town, and a powerful boom shook the buildings. Everyone who had heard the rumors ran outside and looked toward the Christian buildings and yard, thinking that perhaps the wooden god had spoken. Many of those who had joined the Christians decided to leave them because of the clear warning from the most powerful of gods.

While the heavens still rumbled, Holme opened the door of the smithy and stuck his head out. He too hoped that the god had struck the Christians, but there was no smoke to be seen. Holme shook his head, thinking that he'd probably have to do it himself to get rid of the Christians and the destruction they brought. Privately he had always felt that the motionless, wooden gods weren't worth much, but there had been some years of peace for Ausi and him. Now she was being torn again by the old uneasiness; those causing it had to go.

The day before the midwinter sacrifice, Ausi ran into one of the monks, who gestured amiably for her to stop. He said she should come to the Christians' house early the next morning to see and hear what the new god had to offer those who came to him. She should bring her family along, too.

While he talked, he looked wonderingly at the beautiful woman; he knew she was the master smith's wife. Her eyes sparkled, her lips quivered, and she looked around timidly. Then she told him briefly, excitedly, that she had been baptized. A long time ago, over there. She pointed with a supple arm toward the shore.

This wasn't the first time the monk had heard about his predecessor, but it had the same unpleasant effect every time. It must have been a false teacher. He himself was the one God had chosen to be the light in the north. Ausi saw his face darken as she described the stranger who had baptized her, but he didn't respond; he merely repeated that the true and perfect Christ awaited her the next morning. Then he walked on, and Ausi saw him stop a thrall farther down the street.

So it wasn't the stranger who had sent the new monks, she thought with disappointment. But she still wanted to join the Christians; maybe Christ Himself would recognize her. The stranger had once said that not so much as a bird fell to earth without His knowing it, and she was much bigger than a bird. Sometimes she believed Christ had helped them, since everything was going so well, but she didn't dare say so to Holme.

In any case, she had talked with one of the new men now, and even if they weren't like the stranger, they still must know a lot about Christ. She had to know more or she'd never have any peace. If Holme wouldn't let her, she'd have to go behind his back. Maybe she could gradually win Tora over to her side. But the new god and His monks would never get the best of Holme.

Ausi had lain awake since midnight, and when she got up to light the fire, she could still see stars shining through the smoke vent. After a long, uneasy wait, she heard a door slam and steps tramping outside on the hard frozen ground. She knew it was the Christian family from down the street, and she got up and dressed in the feeble light from the fire. She remembered how difficult that would have been to do back when they were thralls, but now that no danger threatened, Holme slept more soundly.

As she sneaked out, Ausi pushed back the thought of what would happen when she returned. Maybe she'd think of something to say before then, or maybe Christ would help since she was doing this for His sake. He could make Holme and Tora keep sleeping.

The houses were still quiet as Ausi walked through the streets, but the smoke was rising denser from the vents where the Christians lived. They were awake. It was cold, and the narrow crescent of the moon hung at an angle above the mainland forest. A dog was barking somewhere on the outskirts of town, and the ice around the island roared as it contracted from the cold.

The Christians' door stood ajar, and it was lighted inside; in the heathen temple, a fire was burning, and there was a smell of burned meat. Some people entered, and Ausi hesitated a moment between the house of Christ and the shrine of the wooden god. If she went into the temple, Holme would be surprised but not enraged; their life would continue peacefully. But strife and danger attended the new god, and everything would be as it had been before.

She was still hesitating between the gates when the Christians' door opened wide, and a voice asked her to come in. She saw the heathens streaming into the temple; then she entered the Christians' house, and the bolt was thrown behind her. Anxious but happy, Ausi was led into the light, and everyone, including the chieftain, recognized her and welcomed her with friendly faces.

The hall was more beautiful than the one the stranger had used a long time ago, but most of the things inside belonged to the chieftain. The most distinguished of the monks said that things would be coming on ships in the spring to enable them to serve their God in a way more worthy of Him. Not that it meant so much; He looked most at the heart. Ausi remembered some Christians returning in surprise with gifts and sacrifices they had tried to offer Christ in return for His help. The monk had told them that He would help them for nothing. Many of them were glad; others didn't believe it and turned back to the wooden gods with their gifts.

Ausi understood more of the monk's words than she had hoped, but it was still strange that He who ruled all things and was the strongest of all gods had sent His servants on foot and unarmed. She had heard that they would cry frequently and abuse themselves. That was partly why Holme and many others despised them. They should be like Holme, powerful and manly, and everything would be easier to understand.

Sporadic shouts and murmurs came through the smoke vent, and Ausi realized that the main sacrifice had begun across the yard. Once they heard a loud scornful laugh, and many of the Christians stopped listening to what the monk was saying and turned in terror to the door. The monk seemed not to notice until the uproar threatened to drown him out, at which point his voice rose, his face grew lighter, and he almost looked happy about what was going on outside. The chieftain, however, looked sternly toward the door, wrinkling his forehead and twitching his beard.

Not many could join in the Christians' singing once the monk had stopped talking. The song to the wooden gods consisted mostly of loud yells intermingled with prayers for help in danger or for a good harvest. The tumult outside kept mounting, and suddenly there was a loud crash against the door. Ausi trembled, thinking of Holme. He was probably out there; the rock had probably flown from his hand.

When the service was over and the monk had held his hands over them, the chieftain opened the door. The space separating the houses of the gods was packed with people who grew quiet as they saw the door open. The chieftain spoke angrily and ordered the people outside to make room for the Christians. He took the lead himself, clearing a path between two ranks of heathens who were more threatening now with their silence than with the noise they had made before.

Ausi walked with downcast eyes but sensed someone step out of the crowd and walk behind her. When she turned onto a side street, the heavy steps followed, but neither spoke. Once again she realized that all gods were powerless against Holme, both the old ones and the new one.

From the church door the monk watched his little congregation disperse and disappear. They were nothing compared to the remaining mob of heathens. Everywhere, pillars of smoke from the sacrificial feast jutted into the cold green sky. The sun would soon rise and the pagans would take this as a sign of the wooden gods' victory over Christ. Here nature itself was against Him.

The heathens stared at the monk silently, a sea of clear eyes and long beards. Their anger was gone, and he marveled at this strange people in their wintry land. They could seize and kill him, but instead they went their ways, finally leaving the yard empty. Only a few figures continued to move around the crude idol on the other side.

A moment later, the monk saw the hills filled with people facing east. The blood-red sliver of the sun rose through the cold haze on the horizon, and a strange shout erupted from a thousand throats. As he walked away, he could hear the sun worshipers' loud, monotonous songs.

The chieftain had warned the foreigners not to show themselves that day or night. The tumultuous morning was nothing compared to what could happen during the evening's raucous eating and drinking. Many would surely vow to kill the foreigners during the year that would begin after the midwinter sacrifice. But the monks refused to shut themselves in; their lives were in someone else's hands.

After the people had greeted the sun, they disappeared into their homes, and the town fell silent. On the far side of the island, smoke rose from the king's farmstead. It was a cold, quiet, and hard land, and the people were just like it. The monk's work had scarcely begun. For a moment, as though in a vision, he saw the hundreds of years that it would take, the infinitesimal impact he would have. The ancient empire of the wooden gods was standing against him.

In the spring when the ice would neither support you nor break up, the store of grain ran out, and the townspeople had to live on fish and meat for several days. But the same day the bluish-white, glittering ice floes heaved splashing and roaring against the shore, numerous sails approached at a good clip before a heavy wind.

Ausi and her daughter heard feet running, and looking outside, they saw people, old, young, and children, rushing to the harbor. They also saw the king's familiar black and yellow sail on the lake.

Mother and daughter quickly closed up their house and ran after the others. They raced past the smithies, lifting their skirts high, and saw Holme with his smiths gathered around him. He yelled angrily at them for their curiosity, and the smiths laughed. The daughter smiled back at them, her black hair flying in the wind. Tora passed her mother and reached the harbor before her. Holme watched them, his anger turning to pride when the smiths praised them both.

The Christian priests stood a short distance behind the mass of people in the harbor, so Ausi could get a good look at them. They tensely watched the first ship with its golden dragon head and talked softly in their mother tongue. You could already make out the king standing among his warriors. He nodded and smiled, and the crowd buzzed animatedly in response.

Behind the warships came a row of boats loaded with grain. The barricade was raised and the boats tied up at the dock, one beside the other. While the king talked with the town leaders, hundreds of inhabitants crowded around the boats with baskets, and the sale began. By the time Ausi returned with her bushel, the hand mills were already clattering in many houses. The king's men stood up to their knees in the yellow grain they were measuring out from the boats.

After the king, the chieftain, and both monks had walked back to town, Ausi and her daughter stood looking at the ships. Ausi noticed a young man or boy on one of them, staring at her and Tora. He had wicked, blue eyes, and his head was bent forward as if a weight sat on his neck. He was almost as tall as the men, but he seemed more like an overgrown child. He stared at Tora with intense, scornful interest. Uneasy, Ausi picked up her basket and left, holding her daughter by the hand. She looked back a couple of times and saw the strange figure silhouetted against the sky.

For several days she thought about the peculiar boy and his stare. He must presage some evil that would befall her or her daughter. Nothing could happen to Holme—hardened to misfortune, he was always the strongest.

Ausi was concerned about Holme for another reason. He hadn't said a word about her attending the Christians' worship service; he just cautioned her not to do it again. But she could tell he was up to something against the Christians, and many people supported him, the thralls most of all. They would walk through fire and water for him if they had to. Holme associated with thralls as equals, and he didn't hide the fact that he had once been a thrall himself. He constantly worked to make things better for them. No one in town any longer dared whip a thrall in front of Holme. This had happened on two occasions, and both times the consequences had been grave.

The most distinguished of the two monks walked among the thousands of green burial mounds, while the spring sun shone on his gray cape and drawn face. It was totally silent; only an occasional puff of wind moved through the grass on the sides of the mounds and softly rustled delicate birch leaves. The monk looked out over the mounds and thought with sorrow about the thousands of heathen souls burning in the eternal fires while their bodies rested in this idyllic place. For a moment, he thought their punishment for ignorance was too severe, but he pushed the thought away, putting it in God's hands. Perhaps on the Day of Judgment, He would be moved by mercy, and walk among the mounds, calling up the stern, bearded men, the self-assured women, and the guiltless children from the graves. Perhaps He would give them a chance to enter His kingdom.

From one of the tallest mounds, the monk looked down at the town and the water glistening brightly beyond it. Many disappointments had been prepared for him; still, his work had begun. Soon a ship would come with everything they needed to hold more worthy and dignified worship services. The heathens were like children; they believed only in demonstrations of power, wanted to see glitter and hear songs and music. They didn't believe in empty hands and meek promises.

Through the silence came distant, melodic sounds from town—ringing blows from the smithies, tapping and scraping from the craftsmen's sheds, songs and shouting from the harbor. The distance refined the sounds, blending them together with the soft whispering wind and the songs of birds. God had given the pagans a beautiful land; someday they would realize that and be filled with gratitude.

The monk noticed there were more ships in the harbor than usual; that meant a business journey to a foreign land. He knew what kind of business the heathens conducted on their journeys— he had run into them himself. That's why he had come to the heathen land empty-handed, and that's why his work had been obstructed. They were thieves, not merchants.

Perhaps resistance would lessen after enough of the most headstrong warriors had sailed away. It would be good if a storm destroyed their ships or enemies defeated them. Then the heathens would be enraged at the wooden gods and turn to Christ. On the other hand, they might think that Christ had provoked their gods into sending misfortune upon their people.

Still mulling that over, the monk left the mounds and walked to the city gate. He had to step aside for a line of people carrying a corpse toward the mounds. It was an old man, and the sun lit up his silver beard against the yellow skin. His head rocked slightly from the motion of the pallbearers. Behind him came a man carrying the dead man's tools and the food he would need for the journey. The Christian monk watched the procession and prayed silently for the old heathen's soul; then he walked through the gate.

Between the defense works and town lay an untouched meadow where the children could play. The monk passed a group of children sitting on the ground, and he stopped, marveling at their play. They sat in rows; the biggest boy stood in front of them, holding something in his hand. Meadow blossoms and cowslips danced around him in the gentle breeze. The monk stared at what the boy was holding and thought the devil was playing a trick on him. He rubbed his eyes and looked again. What the heathen boy had, and what the northern sun was shining on, was a book, perhaps one he had lost on the journey.[6]

The monk walked over and stretched out his hand; the boy gave him the book. The children watched him silently as he examined it and asked them where they had gotten it. It was in bad shape, but it was one of his, stolen by pirates. Over fathomless roads, it had found him after a winter and spring.

Clutching the book to his chest, he told the children to visit him

6. Rimbert reports that Ansgar and Witmar were plundered "of nearly forty books which they had accumulated for the service of god" (*Anskar*, chapter 10, pp. 47–48), but not that they retrieved any of them.

at the chieftain's house for a reward; the boy nodded sullenly. He surely couldn't think the foreign plaything was worth much. But how could the children pretend to hold a Christian worship service—where had they seen one? It had to be the first Bible ever in town, perhaps in the whole heathen land. The book's inherent power had probably taken hold of the children and given them the idea.

The monk felt infused with new strength when he saw God's printed word. He didn't need to know how it had reached him; he could see the hand behind it and that gave him new powers. Soon he would have other books, but this one would always be dearest. It had been returned to him by the hand of God.

The sunshine was dazzling, and the various sounds from town contained light and hope. That evening he would call his little congregation together and share some of the extraordinary news. Everything could move forward more quickly now.

A dark, powerful figure like a fragment of the night walked past on the cross street in front of him, and a vague sense of danger emanated from it. For a moment, he felt his new joy subdued. The silent master smith was his and the congregation's most dangerous enemy, a Saul of the north, but a miracle could happen, even with him. His wife hadn't returned since the midwinter sacrifice, but the work had begun in her; you could see that in her restless look. Surely she must have been mistaken when she spoke indignantly about having been baptized a long time ago.

Summer was coming to the heathen land, and before it was over, the church must be well established. Then he could return to his homeland and witness before God and king that he had completed his task.

A few days later the monk went to the harbor to watch the ships sail. The entire town was there, the warriors' families standing closest to the dock. Many of them would never see their husbands, fathers, or sons again. The warriors ranged in age from adolescents with sparse beards to grim, gray-bearded adults. The sacrificial fires had burned all night so the gods would favor the journey, but the Christian monk beseeched Christ to bring down storm and devastation. The weather was still favorable, though, with sun and a fresh breeze.

Work had stopped throughout town; no sounds came from the smithies or sheds. The monk observed a weeping wife hang a small cross around her husband's neck to protect him on the perilous journey. But he had seen many such crosses, and they didn't fool him anymore. They didn't represent the cross of Christ but a hammer, the weapon of the most powerful wooden god.

The monk stood there until the ships were far away, their golden dragons glowing against the blue waves capped with white. When he finally returned to town, the families were still standing there. The smell of the sacrifices was everywhere, and once again the monk petitioned Christ to send a ruinous storm against the Viking fleet to demonstrate His superiority over the wooden gods. Many of His staunchest opponents were gone, and the work could accelerate. But the black-haired Saul was still standing in the way; maybe the hand of God would strike him down.

Even as he thought, the first blows resounded from the smithies. Black smoke and sparks rose from the roof vents, and the bellows creaked. The monk took the road past Holme's house and looked at the snake-adorned door fittings. Once he had asked the chieftain to drive Holme from town, but the chieftain, the town's most powerful man besides the king, didn't dare. He was afraid that the smiths, the craftsmen, and the masses of thralls would riot if he laid hands on the master smith. They all considered Holme their chieftain and protector, and they did everything he asked.

The monk had stopped in front of the ornamented door, but when he saw two female figures coming up the street, he walked on. He had wanted to talk with the smith's wife, but should Holme happen to come home no one knew what might happen. Smiling, the monk shook his head at that thought—was he afraid of the smith now, too? Yes. He didn't want to die yet, but once the work had a firm foundation, he wouldn't back down.

A group of women, old men, and children were standing on the point, watching the ships. The breeze played in the women's clothes and the old men's beards. The wooden god stood in the shrine, the corners of his mouth drawn up as if he smiled scornfully at the servant of Christ.

The chieftain's wife labored with other women thralls in the foreign land, digging up the ground for their master. Her face was gray and angry; no one would guess that she had once been a chieftain's wife and had herself ruled over thralls.

Two days had passed since they had first seen smoke rising beyond the forest; the day before it had come closer, and today the smell of it was riding on the wind. The first survivors arrived that afternoon, saying the invaders spared no one. Those who valued their lives had to flee to the woods or to town for protection within its walls.

With inner glee, the chieftain's wife had watched the smoke drawing closer and closer. She hoped her countrymen were on their way. She had once heard two men speaking her language when they visited the master, but she had been locked away and couldn't be heard herself. Perhaps her liberation was moving through the forest from the west. In the confusion, she would try to stay behind when the others left.

But in the late afternoon when the smoke began to rise from the neighboring farmstead across the woods, no one thought about forcing her to leave with them. There was a wave and a shout from the yard, and the women rushed back, all except the two kidnapped women. The nearly grown daughter had already raced off, a young thrall clutching her hand. When she saw her mother remaining behind, she turned back a few steps, waving and calling, but the older woman stood peacefully by her former mistress's side. The girl hesitated, looked around for the young thrall who was frantically waving for her, and then gave up her mother and ran toward safety with him.

Shouting and commotion came from the farmstead; a wagon was wheeled up and loaded with the most valuable possessions. The thralls had chased off the cows and pigs as they fled. Smoke billowed in waves above the forest, and an indeterminate clamor rose from it. The thrall girl's mother suddenly had a change of heart and began running after the fleeing people.

They were still in sight when the thieves came swarming out of the forest on horseback and on foot. They stopped at the forest's edge, looking suspiciously at the silent farmstead that blocked the fleeing people from view. They saw the woman standing fearlessly in the middle of the field, and they looked about in all directions as if they expected an ambush.

"Bring the witch here," the chieftain ordered, and two men walked toward the farmstead. The woman came forward to meet them, and they brought her back, surprised she spoke their language. The chieftain sat down on a rock, gestured toward another for the woman, and listened as she told her story, energetically pointing and gesticulating in her happiness.

A tall, grizzled warrior paid closer, more eager attention to her than the others did. As she described the attack, the burning, and the kidnapping, he nodded as if he knew all about it and was invigorated by what she said. But he said nothing.

After the chieftain had heard the woman out, he went to the farmstead with his army. They searched the buildings, but everything of value was gone. Some provisions were carried out and laid at a distance from the buildings. When all was ready, Geire walked up to the chieftain and asked if he could light the fire.

"Why?"

"He burned my farmstead."

"So burn his," the chieftain said without further ado.

The woman sat down in the grass, and her eyes shone with happiness when the farmstead began to burn. The warriors sat down, too. Some fetched water for the bread they had found. The youngest of them, a deformed boy, moved as close as he could get to the fire as he ate his bread. His head was bowed under an invisible burden. Suddenly the woman caught sight of him through the smoke and hurried toward him.

"Svein!" she screamed shrilly, but the youth didn't look at her. She rushed up, grabbed him, and spun him around. The rows of seated warriors looked up in surprise as they ate.

The woman hugged the youth, scrutinizing his eyes, nose, and hands. Then, as she felt his neck, Svein shoved her violently away, screaming in rage, "What do you want from me, you old hag?"

The warriors began laughing but stopped abruptly when Geire walked up to the pair, put his hand out to the woman, and murmured something that made the boy stare at her in surprise from beneath a lowered forehead. Then the three of them sat apart from the others while the farmstead burned. Geire happened upon a tool in the field and threw that into the fire too so everything would be consumed. They had been avenged by fire now; maybe they could catch the survivors and complete their revenge with the sword.

At midsummer, the families in the island town vainly watched and waited for their marauding ships to return. Some approached Christ, asking Him to bring the ships home; others sacrificed almost everything they had to the wooden gods. Autumn came, but they still continued to hope. Wintering in a foreign, conquered land was not unusual.

The Christian congregation hadn't grown as much as the monks had hoped. They had the things they needed now for a worship service. Two bells, a big one and a small one, rang out crisply over the island and surrounding water. The blackened smiths stood in the doorway, listening and laughing at the new gimmick. In the summer night, a heathen fisherman rested on his oars as he listened in half-terror to the strange clear tones bounding across the water. But no one heeded their call to come to Christ.

The monks had to admit that the Christianity of the pagans they had managed to convert wasn't worth much. All they wanted were the advantages; their hearts were cold and indifferent before the blood of the Cross. To them the Cross was a simple, carved god, and they saw blood much too often for it to make any impression. Without daily guidance, they would soon slide back into darkness. Many of them would leave the worship service and go to their household god, sacrificing to him for help with what Christ couldn't or wouldn't do. The monks sensed the boundlessness of their field of labor.

They could see clearly how small their congregation was one

spring day when they left for their homeland.[7] The lake had just opened, and the last thin ice floes were clanking against the rocks on shore. A big ship had come for them, and many realized then that the priests must be men of high station in their homeland. But no one cared about that here.

The Christians clustered at the front of the small harbor gathering; behind stood the crowds of heathens, come to see the departure. Holme watched with his smiths from the hill where he had once torn down the church. The foundation stones were still there, half sunk into the ground. The smiths could view the whole harbor. Holme knew his wife and daughter were down there and thought he could see them next to the Christians. The whole time the bells clanged anxious, hasty peals.

Before the vessel was rowed out, the most distinguished monk stood on the prow, lifted his hands into the air, and in a loud clear voice delivered his followers into God's hands. The heathens were totally silent, and the smiths could hear some of his words. Holme smiled grimly, confident that when they were gone, everyone would return to the old ways.

From the vessel, the departing monk, tears streaming down his face, watched his congregation on the shore. Some of the women cried; others waved; the men raised their arms in a gesture of farewell. The children played obliviously, clambering over the pilings. The old chieftain, whom they had to thank for whatever success they had achieved, was standing in front. As the vessel moved farther out, the monk could see the entire town. The sun was shining on the yellowish-green sod roofs, and the wind was driving the smoke eastward. A few figures, black against the yellow-green background, were standing on a rise. When he saw them he had a

7. Ansgar and Witmar spent a total of a year and a half on this mission (*Anskar*, chapter 12, p. 49).

sudden premonition that his work was not secure; he thought of the powerful enemies he had in town. The monks had felt Holme's hostility in various ways. Many agreed with him.

No doubt many in the congregation would fall back into paganism. As soon as something went wrong, Christ would take the blame, and they would return to their wooden idols. Christ faced an ancient army of blood-smeared wooden gods in these northern heathen lands.

Thin, dirty cows and goats were grazing on the shores. Once a few horn blasts blared from the woods. The town was still visible, and the monk could distinguish the bell tower and the bells. When he got to his homeland, he would continue to send the chieftain items for the worship service until the new monks arrived to carry on the good work.

He had been the first of God's messengers to come to this luminous and beautiful, but difficult, land. They had probably had Christian thralls there for a long time, and he had heard vague rumors about a man who supposedly had come through the woods on foot, spoken God's words, and baptized people by the shore. But there was no further trace of him, and once those heathens who still remembered him had gone, he would never be mentioned again. He undoubtedly was one of the many deluded souls who had been wrong about God's call. Most of them never reached their destination; instead God allowed the heathens to kill them en route so they'd be spared an even worse fate. His own unmistakable sign had been God's saving him from the hands of the pirates and guiding him to his goal—the remote heathen town on the island.

A cloud had risen quickly in the west, and when the monk caught his last glimpse of the town, it was in shadow. In that instant, the distant bells rang irregularly, anxiously, and then fell silent. Did that mean the wooden gods would reclaim their town entirely? The wind mounted and large, wet flakes of snow flew along on it. The Frisians' vessel picked up speed, white water foaming around the prow. Had heathens been on board, they would have believed their gods were blowing the Christians away from their land, and their faith in the gods would have grown still stronger.

Islets and isthmuses that moments before had been bathing in the spring light on the blue water turned sullen and dark, and the swirling spring snow colored their northern sides a gray white. The ship soon entered an area where a current flowed on both sides of an islet. On the north end, a long gravel ridge thrust up, its slopes covered with woods, its crown bare; on the south side the water slammed against lofty, precipitous gray cliffs. Some fishermen were busy on the shores, and some boats lay tied to a log landing on the sides sheltered from the wind. But the monk's God did not allow him to see the powerful Christian town and many churches that one day would stand there.[8]

The sleet turned to a cold rain, and he sought shelter, his heart troubled and heavy because of his departure.

The ship was still in sight and the people were still standing in the harbor when Holme and the smiths walked up toward the Christian buildings and yard. No one was there except the free thrall ringing the bells. The thrall looked as though he felt important and satisfied with the sound he was creating as the bells swung on their pole.

But as the dark group approached, the sound quickened, becoming more anxious than before. The bell ringer knew perfectly well what the master smith and the others thought of the Chris-

8. I.e., Stockholm.

tians, and he was alone. A distance away, they started picking up stones, and when the first came whizzing, the bell ringer let go the rope and ran toward the town gate. The smiths' laughter pursued him, and he heard the smaller bell ring out a shrill cry when a stone hit it.

The smiths walked up to the bell tower and shook it, but didn't tear it down. The mass of people in the harbor began dispersing, and the chieftain might come any minute. Violence toward the Christians and their possessions wouldn't go over well in broad daylight; the king and the chieftain protected them. But the opportunity would come soon enough.

From the heathen shrine, a couple of the wooden god's servants delighted in watching the smiths. The wooden god himself peered rigidly ahead with his crooked, scornful smile. Stripes of darkened blood from the spring sacrifice stained him. The smiths looked at him respectfully, but Holme cared as little about him as he did about Christ. Holme had never sacrificed to any god, and no god had ever helped him either. He had made his own way, and that's what he would always do.

When the chieftain appeared, provoked by the bell ringer's story, the smiths were already gone and everything was still. He didn't dare go to the smithies to make them answer for this. The smiths had their own understanding of law and justice. It wasn't far to their sledgehammers and axes when they needed them, and it did no good to talk with their grim leader. He was born a thrall, and a thrall he remained—a difficult and dangerous thrall chieftain.

When Geire, Svein, and his mother stepped ashore below their burned settlement one day in the late summer, they saw a couple of gray-haired figures stumbling and hobbling toward the forest through the open area. The new arrivals moved cautiously up the slope, keeping their weapons ready, but all they found were two half-grown pigs that let out a terrified guttural squeal, wheeled around, and fled in a waddling gallop.

The mounds of ashes had been nearly leveled by the year's rain and wind, and were almost overgrown with grass and shrubs, but among the trees stood a little hut made of sticks and mud. The old men had fled from it. Barley was growing in a couple of small fields, and a narrow path had been worn between them and the buildings. The charred wooden god, turned a shimmering gray by wind and weather, stood on the slope. The woman recognized him but paid no attention. He hadn't been able to stop the misfortune that befell the settlement and its people.

The three sat resting at the settlement after checking the hut. There were no valuables inside; everything had probably burned. The old men who had fled to the forest were surely nearby, but they didn't look dangerous.

From where they sat, they had a view of the three large mounds in the burial grounds, and they talked nostalgically about the last man who had been put there and about the good years they had when he was alive. They talked about Holme and Ausi too, but the woman's face contorted with hate and rage, and she admonished her brother and son to take revenge if they ever found those two alive. She suspected Holme had shown the invaders to the farmstead. When it came to sorcery, he knew more than most people did.

Geire listened, and as she talked, he began to call the thrall back to mind. He remembered him now as the master of the largest smithy in town, who had given Svein a new sword to replace the burned one. He also remembered Svein's strange fear of the smith. Soon everything was clear to him.

If his sister was right, the worst of the revenge remained to be exacted. The gods had helped them find the invaders' farmsteads in the unknown land; many had fallen in the battle, some had been taken prisoner, and he had cut some down with his sword when they defiantly affirmed they had burned and harried where he was now sitting. If the black-haired smith was behind it all, he would answer for it with his life.

When they walked on, they saw a little mound of earth where the grass had not yet taken root. They didn't know that the old woman thrall was resting there—Stor and Tan had buried her early that summer. She had her spindle-whorl with her, a couple of needles, a pair of scissors, and a clay bowl with meat and bread in it. Since then, the old men talked about their greatest worry— who would prepare them for their final journey?

They hadn't recognized the three visitors. As they had many times before, they hid among the trees, anxiously and fearfully sticking their bristly gray snouts out. No one stayed at the burned settlement long; the menacing wooden god stood on his stone, ruling over the solitude and desolation, and the place just usually wasn't as fit for human habitation as it should be.

After stopping at the edge and looking back at what had once been their home, the three proceeded into the woods. They agreed they would rebuild it when the time came, and it wouldn't hurt anything for a couple of old outlaws to keep up parts of the fields. There were good forest meadows in the area, and the chieftain's wife wanted to rest a while beside her first husband. She didn't care about the second one with the spindly legs. He probably had never been buried. No doubt wild animals had eaten him once they dared brave the heat after the invaders had dragged her off and Svein had run into the forest.

Late in the summer, a rumor went around town that the two Christians who had gone home in the spring had sent two replacements. The new ones had received permission to do whatever they wanted to spread the teaching of the new god.[9]

But another rumor came from the fields and meadows, from the large farmsteads and the small clearings in the forest, that the wooden gods were more incensed than ever before. The fertility god had loosed a disease on the grain, a black blight that rode the wind, devouring the grain in its path. Instead of loaded grain boats, famine would sweep grinning down on the town from the forests and flatlands. The heathens scornfully asked each other what Christ could do about that.

In autumn the townspeople looked vainly toward the mainland for the boats, as their storehouses quickly ran dry. Soon people spoke openly, claiming that the misery had to be caused by the new god. Some people could see clear signs of the wooden gods' wrath.

Many took their boats to distant farmsteads seeking grain, but there was none to be found. The farmers held onto whatever they could of the miserable harvest. A royal decree to sell the extra grain was received with scorn, axes, and swords. Then one day, a large ship loaded with grain came to the Christians from their homeland.

The smithies and craftsmen's sheds gradually fell silent. No one was willing to exchange grain and meat for tools or weapons. Many had left the town for the farmsteads of relatives or for for-

9. Louis the Pious arranged for Ansgar to become the first archbishop of Hamburg, with all of Scandinavia under his jurisdiction, and Ansgar in turn consecrated his nephew Gautbert as bishop of Sweden. Gautbert then went to Sweden with his companion, Nithard, to carry on the mission work. (*Anskar,* chapter 16, p. 57).

eign lands, trying to find something to sustain them. The pigs no longer grubbed in the streets; the dogs ran around emaciated and half-crazed, and their famished howls rose loudly toward the sky at night. Many had sacrificed the last of their household animals to the wooden gods, but they stared ahead grimly, unmoved. Among the heathens a murmur of hate was born and grew—the Christians had to go or everyone would perish. Those who owned thralls drove them off so they wouldn't deplete the already sparse provisions. Starving thralls were slinking everywhere; panting, they crawled into the forest, stuffing berries into their mouths with cupped hands, digging up roots and picking bitter acorns. During the frosty nights, they would make their way to town and hunch close to the building walls to keep warm.

But everyone knew the Christians had grain.

When Holme could no longer stand the silent pleas in his wife's and daughter's eyes, he walked to town. Their drawn faces followed him beseechingly; they were used to his always finding a way. Holme couldn't live on roots and berries anymore; he had a wild craving for a loaf of bread or a piece of meat.

For several nights he had searched near the Christians' building trying to find something from their storeroom, but it was well protected and there was always a guard. He wasn't alone on his nightly prowls; dark figures sneaked around him, looking hungrily at the stout building that held the grain.

After Holme had given all he could give, he preferred spending the days inside. When the starving thralls saw him, they hurried up with hope-filled eyes, but he drove them away in despair. Why did they think he could do more than anyone else? He felt more and more responsible for them, even though his look was threatening and his words hard. When the Christian bells rang, he shook his fist at them, remembering Ausi's timidly asking him if she could go to the Christians for a little grain.

This time he hadn't gone far before a couple of homeless thralls started following him, refusing to be put off by his stern demeanor. A group on a street corner noticed and joined them. Holme could hear them tramping along behind him, and their numbers swelled. He felt their trust weighing him down, and he didn't know what to do.

The larger church bell struck hesitantly, and the smaller bell started tinkling along with it. Without knowing why, Holme walked toward the sound, and the silent, plodding group followed him. Others came running up the roads and streets to join them.

Dozens of heathens were already standing outside the Christian yard where the large church building had been begun. They had assorted goods with them and begged the Christians to trade them grain. Holme and the group of thralls stood like a large shadow in the open area, but the Christians could see they were unarmed and paid them no attention.

One of the new Christians told the pagans that anyone who accepted the new teaching would get grain and whatever else he needed. That was the only condition—they weren't selling or bartering anything. The Christians claimed that Christ had sent this misfortune on the heathens to save them and bring them to Himself.

As Holme listened to their words, he noticed a stone font where they would baptize those coming to Christ. There was water in it, and one of the monks stood ready beside it. Holme felt the old defiance and rage, dormant for several years, begin to waken. He looked at the Christians' full cheeks and clear eyes and then at the thralls, standing there, looking like starving dogs, chewing on nothing. He had to get them something to eat, even if it meant risking his security or his life. There he stood with the unarmed thralls, shaking with hunger, while the Christians were well-fed and armed. They would fight for their grain.

Holme watched a woman walk hesitantly over to the Christians, holding her child by the hand. He knew that Ausi would do the same if she dared. Maybe in the end she would anyway. It would be better if the Christians were killed and their buildings burned, even if the chieftain himself was one of them and the buildings belonged to him. Lives were at stake here—he realized that soon his body would no longer obey his will.

The Christians, beginning to get a little nervous about the threatening band of thralls, saw its well-known leader give an order to the thralls, who all disappeared with him toward the smithies. The Christians breathed easier and their voices, offering a bushel of grain per soul, became more relaxed.

Some of the thralls were hoping Holme had bread in his smithy, but what he took out of the chests and down from the walls was nothing to chew on—he brought out axes, swords, knives, and sledgehammers. Holme passed the weapons out among them, thinking that this time someone would be fighting by his side; he had always been alone before.

However, when he stood before the Christian buildings and yard again with his armed thralls, Holme was reluctant to attack. The Christians kept luring people with their grain, while a dull chanting voice from the pagan shrine warned of the wooden gods' further wrath.

While the thralls had gone to get weapons, more women had approached the Christians, among them Holme's wife and daughter. Ausi was chewing greedily, waving for him to come over though she was terrified by what she had done. Tora, eating peacefully and looking out across the open area, didn't seem to understand the price she would have to pay for the bread.

Having taken this all in, Holme ran without a sound toward the Christians; before anyone knew what had happened, he had smashed the baptismal font to bits with his sledgehammer. Water splashed everywhere, and the Christians fled, shrieking in confusion. The thralls gave chase, and then there was chaos. The chieftain was gone, but the Christians ran to his house for protection while the heathens searched for the grain. When everyone was safe inside and the bar was thrown, a window opened, and a voice threatened the thralls with eternal damnation.

Two men stood guard at the storeroom, and one made a valiant effort to defend himself against the thralls. A stick struck the spear from his hand, and another landed on his skull. By then, the other was already at the chieftain's house banging on the door to get in. At the same time, the hatch of the storeroom gave way before Holme's sledgehammer, revealing the golden grain in a huge bin. The thralls leaped into it, stuffing themselves with their hands. The throng outside grew and with it, the cries of hunger from the children with their mothers. People streamed in from town; everyone wanted to be there. No one cared how all this had happened.

Holme tossed the closest thralls aside when he saw the mass of people, and a while later, the Christians could see the pagans coming with bushels and tankards. The master smith stood measuring out equal portions of the grain. Men, women, and children hurried back to their homes, cramming grain into their mouths. It wasn't long before the hand mills and millstones in every hut began clattering. Some of the newly converted Christians had remained outside, and Holme gave them a share even though their hair was still dripping with Christian baptismal water.

Once everything had been handed out, the area was deserted; only a few children were left crawling around, picking up the spilled grain. The larder was empty, and Holme had neglected himself. The Christians saw him stop, looking around with a sledgehammer in one hand and the empty measuring pail in the other. His daughter wanted to run to him, but some of the others restrained her. Ausi stood in silent dread, not knowing what to do. Holme turned his head like a bear and looked up at them before he walked down the street and disappeared.

Ausi heard the Christians around her growling that Holme had forfeited his life by doing what he had done. As soon as the chieftain returned, he'd complain to the king. The hater of Christ—now a murderer and a thief too—would get his punishment from both earthly and heavenly powers.

She saw her daughter glare with raging eyes at those charging her father with these things, and Ausi wished she had stayed home and not come to the Christians. Then Holme would not have forgotten to take his share of the grain for his wife and daughter. But she also wanted to stay with the Christians and learn more about them. If Christ was who they said He was, then, of course, He could forgive Holme for what he had done for the hungry thralls.

The Christians weren't going to starve to death; the monks were already talking about another ship coming from their homeland. Maybe she could hide some food for Holme if she found out where he was. The Christians would become more and more powerful, and Holme would understand someday why she had gone to them.

The Christians' threats that Holme would be punished soon meant nothing to her. Only people who didn't know Holme talked that way. Yet she constantly avoided the anger and accusation in her daughter's eyes.

At a worship service one day, it became clear to Ausi that Christ could have defended Himself against those who hanged Him on the Cross if He had chosen to, and she became very happy. She understood why the stranger had let himself be slaughtered at the spring sacrificial feast so long ago: he wanted to be Christlike. If she had known that before, she could have explained it to Holme though he could never be that way himself. No matter how many men attacked him, he'd fight as long as he could move, and they'd be able to hang him up on a cross only if he were almost dead.

Both the new monks took more interest than their predecessors had in her story about the stranger who had baptized her by the shore many years before. They listened attentively to her description, from the thralldom at the settlement to the great sacrifice when the stranger was hanged in the sacrificial grove together with animals of every size. They shook their heads at Holme's wickedness and said that now he would truly be lost for all time. Christ would strike him down wherever he was hiding. Ausi heard that with a heavy heart, thinking that she had been deceived. A wife should be at her husband's side to the end.

The monks said she should be baptized again; no one could be sure if the stranger had the right to baptize. They had also heard that the master smith had plenty of earthly possessions—she should give some of them for building the church and for her and her daughter's eternal happiness. She thought about the bound chest containing the silver and expensive weapons, the pearls and glass items that Holme had bartered from foreign merchants. Holme should decide all such things, but he was gone and had taken only his weapons with him. The monks would have to wait until she heard from him.

As Ausi saw the gray baptismal font under her bowed head and felt the water dripping in her hair, she wasn't thinking about Christ as she should have been. She was thinking first that the font was smaller than the one Holme had smashed to bits, and she felt some pride over the violence of the sledgehammer blow. Holme always struck hard and straight; no one else was like him.

Then she thought about the summer day when she was first baptized. It was much more beautiful when the stranger stood in the sparkling water, stretching his hand out toward her with a friendly smile. He must have been closer to Christ than those who came after him. She remembered the cross on his chest glittering in the water, but this time she saw only the gray bottom of the font and heard the monk's words repeated over and over again.

But now she could be sure she'd be one of those called up out of the ground when Christ returned. Tora would be baptized too and become one of them. The Christians said that no heathen would be raised, but Holme wasn't aware of that. If he wanted to, he'd get up with or without Christ's help or water on his head.

Tora had watched the baptismal rites with mounting surprise, and Ausi realized she was becoming more and more like her father. Ausi had been ashamed to look Tora in the eye when her turn had come, and when she stood before her daughter with dripping hair, telling her it was her turn, she was asking more than ordering her.

She saw then that Tora was Holme's daughter. Silent but with black, angry disdain in her eyes she looked at both her mother and the monks, who gently called for her.

When coaxing didn't work, a couple of the baptized women grabbed her and dragged her to the font. She fought them fiercely, and one of them screamed out in pain, then displayed a deep bite in her arm, blood oozing from it.

But they couldn't have a heathen in their midst; you had to force a child who didn't understand what was for her own good. Strong arms dragged the panting, furious girl up and held her fast while the water dropped into her black hair. Ausi thought that if Holme had been around, their lives wouldn't have been worth much. When he came back, he would exact hard revenge. With a pang in her heart, she felt that Christ had come between her and her loved ones. Both of them would soon come to loathe her.

After Tora had been baptized, she raced through the door toward their house. Ausi hurried after her, but Tora was already leaving with her few belongings when she arrived. She ignored her mother's plea and ran toward the harbor. She probably intended to go to the mainland to find her father, Ausi thought with great anxiety. It could mean her death; how could she defend herself against wild animals and evil people?

But the harbor was deserted, and the oarsman hadn't seen her daughter. He laughed and said she might have taken a side street to fool her mother. She'd probably come back.

Ausi spent the whole day crying and walking back and forth between harbor and home to see if Tora had returned. She felt great bitterness for Christ and His servants, who had stolen everything dear to her. Why should she rise from the grave on the last day if neither Tora nor Holme could be with her? No, she would rather stay in the earth with them and sleep until the end of time.

The oarsman tried to console her and turned his head in every direction to look for her daughter. A boat had crossed from the other harbor; maybe she was in it. He had rowed Holme across a few days before. When he told her that, his voice took on an admiring tone. A free, rich, and powerful man had never endangered his life, family, and possessions before for the sake of thralls. Holme had saved many from starvation; the grain he had taken from the Christians was still holding out, and it was rumored that several more ships were on the way. No one else would die of hunger now. It was no hardship for the Christians—they had probably hidden grain in several places.

But what the oarsman said did not make Ausi happy. His words reminded her that Holme always thought of himself last; the weak and downtrodden had a powerful protector in him. She had always known that but only thought it natural. Everyone looked to him for help when something went wrong, and he always had advice. But when he had taken that perilous last resort of attacking the Christians and stealing their grain for her, Tora, and the starving thralls, she had turned away from him and stood by the Christians—the Christians who, through their speeches and their invisible white god, had only caused her trouble.

After Holme had paid the oarsman, he headed for the woods the same way he had as a runaway thrall. He wasn't quite sure what to do; he mostly wanted to be by himself to look at the old paths, the old haunts. He wasn't worried about his wife and daughter; no one would harm them, and the Christians would give them whatever they might need. He suspected they had more grain than he had divided up among the starving, homeless thralls.

He was still bitter because Ausi hadn't waited before going to the Christians. That was the first time she hadn't trusted him, and she wasn't the only one who was hungry. It wasn't so bad for Tora—they had hidden away a little food and persuaded her to eat it. This was all because of the Christians and their temptations. Someday he would return and take his revenge, even if he didn't know right now how he would do it.

Toward evening he reached the cave, approaching it cautiously.

Someone or something might be living there, a robber or a wolf. The entrance was too small for a bear.

Everything was quiet; the stillness of the summer ruled in the forest. The marshland still lay below the ridge as before, and a mist hung brooding over it. Stenulf's burial mound had sunk and shrunk. Before Holme left the next day, he'd put a stone on the mound so everyone would know it was a grave. He shuddered at the thought of spending the night so close to the warrior he had killed and put in the mound himself. Stenulf probably wasn't there anymore; he had moved on, doubtlessly. He hadn't had any provisions for the journey, but a warrior like Stenulf would get along well enough without them.

Holme's legs were shaking from the day's journey, and he realized how long he had survived on berries and roots. He remembered that wild strawberries grew on the mossy pile of rocks, and he climbed up to look. They were still there, large forest strawberries so ripe they were almost black. They had vanished from the glades and along the roads a long time ago.

The cave hadn't changed except for the old moss bed where he had slept with Ausi, and where she had later borne the child who froze to death in the forest. The bed had almost moldered away, so he carried in fresh moss before lying down.

Through the door, he could hear an evening wind in the forest, and he thought about how strange it all was. Everything was just like it had been before; all the years he had spent as a smith in town seemed unreal. Perhaps he had been asleep in the cave conjuring them in a dream. Though everything seemed dark to him, he felt more secure in the cave than anyplace else. He'd be an outlaw now after what he had done to the Christians, and the cave was the best place of refuge and defense for him.

For a moment he thought about Christ and His servants. Anyone could see how weak He was; He couldn't even protect His own grain. At least you could see the wooden gods. There they stood—stock-still, staring. Since you couldn't see Christ, He must not exist. How could a nonexistent god help or punish anyone? Ausi and all the others who had gone to the Christians must be simpleminded.

He'd go back someday, and then there'd be trouble. The first Christian stranger had tried to burn the temple of the wooden gods at the great festival of sacrifice, but he had failed and ended up hanging in a tree. Perhaps the Christian buildings would burn a little easier.

His last sensation was an intense longing for home. He thought about his daughter and the harm that might befall her, and his breathing deepened with rage. He decided to slip back one night soon to check on things. Anyone who had hurt her wouldn't live to see the sun rise.

Then Holme calmed down a little, realizing that the smiths and thralls would protect her. He knew too, now that his fatigue wasn't so great, that Tora wouldn't stay with the Christians long. She probably hadn't even realized where her mother was taking her. Maybe he should have taken her with him.

It was quiet outside; only the occasional hoarse bark of a fox broke the silence. There was no sound from either of the ones he had killed near the cave—no heavy steps from Stenulf, no crying from the baby who had frozen to death in the woods. Holme put his weapons within reach and fell asleep, the darkness erasing the entrance to the cave.

The marshland had firmed up quite a bit in the years Holme had been away. He didn't have to venture on rocking tufts anymore, but the shovel-winged birds were still either flying around him with nervous shrieks or skittering between the tufts.

He headed out at first light to reach the settlement before anyone was up. He wanted to look it over in the open. He didn't know what else he wanted to do yet. He might run across something to eat near the settlement, and then he would find a way out. He felt dizzy from hunger now and then, and the green tufts shifted in front of his feet.

Numerous memories followed him on the road or called to him from the forest. For a long time, Ausi and he had talked of returning to the settlement now that they were safe and secure, to freshen their memories about all that had happened there. Neither had expected they'd be separated; now he came alone, fleeing, and on foot, and everything seemed to be in the distant past. The life of an outlaw was all that was left for him.

He reached the settlement just before sunrise. Even before he got there, he knew things had changed; he had noticed that the cow trail to the settlement hadn't been used in years. Animals never gave up their trails. But these were all grown over, and there were no animal smells in the air.

Holme froze in bewilderment, staring across the empty space where grass and shrubs had covered the ashes of the buildings. He sensed a building nearby, but he couldn't see it from the edge of the forest.

An almost imperceptible path ran past the mounds of ashes to the lake. But there was no boat, and the path was little used. He followed it cautiously a while then stopped and saw with surprise the crude and charred wooden god on the stone. He recognized it despite the great change. Who had put it there? What was it guarding?

He also saw fresh pig tracks on the slope, and hunger screamed inside him. Maybe he could find an animal to kill and eat. There were probably some wild ones around that had once lived at the settlement.

He looked toward the old pigsty and saw the sod roof was still there with its grass and tall flowers. Curious, he walked closer and heard muffled grunts. When he opened the door he heard a louder barking sound, and three skinny pigs, a big one and two small ones, blinked at him with terrified white eyes.

Over the years a clump of trees had grown up on three sides of the little hut that Stor and Tan had built and almost hid it completely, much to the old thralls' satisfaction. They thought the wooden god on the stone was helping them, so they offered him thanks by putting food on the stone. As soon as they were out of sight, the forest birds diligently plucked up the offering.

Many forest wanderers, wild and dangerous with hunger, had passed close by, but most of them had moved on without catching sight of the hut. One day at dusk, a famished woodsman had grabbed one of the smaller pigs, but the old men had heard the squeals and rushed over. The thief didn't look dangerous, so they attacked him with their sticks, knocking him unconscious. After a while, he crawled away, moaning. This time, they hadn't been awakened by the pigs' squeals. But when Stor woke up and looked at the blue sky through the vent, he saw what appeared to be a light smoke passing over it. They hadn't had a fire since last night, and those were no morning clouds; it was smoke gliding just over their roof.

He woke up Tan, and the old men cautiously opened the door. They could smell smoke but couldn't see a fire. A soft breeze was passing over the settlement. They sneaked through the grove to get a better look at the yard and slope.

They almost fell over each other in their first terror. A vision from their worst nightmares was standing before them. A little fire was burning in the yard, and beside it stood a mighty, dark figure—the man they feared more than anyone else and who meant certain death for them. One of the small pigs lay slaughtered and skewered next to him, and he seemed to be cooking part of it. He didn't hear them and didn't move. The old thralls withdrew their quivering faces from the foliage, sneaked back to their hut, and barred the door as quietly as they could.

Eyes filled with terror, they squinted at each other in total silence all morning long, hoping the hut wouldn't be discovered. Maybe the god on the stone would help them. They heard the pigs squeal when it was time for them to root in the forest, and several times they heard their enemy coughing and grumbling. They couldn't see the smoke anymore, and soon the sun shone through the smoke vent. The old men stared at the encouraging ray of light and hoped that everything would be all right. Finally, they dared to open the door and listen; they couldn't hear anything except the grunting of pigs, the slow whispering of the forest, and the lapping of the waves.

When they sneaked out among the young trees again, the yard was empty and the fire had gone out. They stood there a long time, poking their beards through the leaves, then inching forward, constantly on the alert. The pig was gone, but a pool of blood showed where it had lost its life. They mumbled to each other that only Holme could have done that without making the pigs squeal. Their peace and safety was gone now. He'd come back as long as there was something to eat. They knew about the famine even though they'd gotten along well themselves because of their stinginess.

In any case, they had seen their deadly enemy again and they were still alive. That cheered them, and, grinning, they let the pigs into the forest, then turned to find something to eat themselves. Suddenly they froze like the wooden god on the stone. Among the young trees between them and the hut stood Holme, holding a long-handled ax and looking at them. They realized in terror that he had been watching them all along.

When the ominous figure approached, Tan started to run but Holme said something so surprising that it stopped him in his tracks. In a soft voice he said that he had no intention of killing them or doing them any harm, and he set the ax against a stone to prove it. The old thralls looked fearful and dubious and didn't answer him. Why had he come if not to hurt them?

But he spoke strange, grave words about how things had changed, and he asked them what had happened to the settlement and its inhabitants. The old men gradually stopped trembling and mumbled to each other, not understanding a thing. Was Holme toying with them, enjoying their agony, or was he going to let them live?

But Holme wasn't remembering the contempt he once had felt for the two fawning, spineless thralls. They were alone and old now and had a right to stay and fend for themselves. But the settlement was big and well-situated; more than just a couple of old men should make use of it.

He had always longed to come back even though he had lived a wretched life as a thrall here. Everything was different; he could stay and rebuild the settlement. The old thralls wouldn't have it any better now, no matter where they might go. Maybe he could bring Tora and Ausi here, that is, if the Christians hadn't won them over completely. Since the relatives' farmstead was deserted and burned too, surely no one would come to claim this land.

He could tell that Stor and Tan didn't like him and would much rather see him go. When he talked with them, they exchanged terrified and angry glances. After so many years, they felt like they owned the settlement. But most of the fields lay fallow, and they had only the two pigs. A strong man with a wife and children should come here—someone who could carve wood and forge new tools and weapons. For a start, he could fix some of the things he had seen lying in a ravine.

He got up from the rock and walked to the cleft where he had once had his smithy. The sod-covered, birch-bark roof had caved in, but the support, red with rust, poked out of the debris. He would clean the place up so the sledgehammer could resound once more.

Stor and Tan, still sitting on the slope, had moved closer to each other; he could see their beards flapping as they mumbled and whispered. They weren't too pleased with the visitor, but that didn't matter. Things would be no worse for them; they would still have their freedom and their harvest. Once the settlement came to life again, everyone there, both men and women, would be free. Holme had been a thrall himself and didn't want to see other thralls around him.

He was out in the forest the same day searching out suitable trees. Stor and Tan could hear his ax, and they rolled their eyes treacherously, clutching the handles of theirs with veined fists. The wooden god on the stone received offerings all day, and they mumbled a prayer for help in their undertaking. He had once been protector of the whole settlement; maybe he'd help them against its (and their) greatest enemy.

The old dead woman's bench was empty so Holme lay down on it. All three of them ate pork that evening, and the old men fetched salt from its hiding place whining all the while about how little they had left and how close they had come to starving several times.

Later they were in an extremely good mood; they vied with each other in complimenting Holme and trying to be his friend. They had hated the old masters as much as he had and thought he had done the right thing by throwing a rock at their son. Now he'd spend his whole life peering at the ground as if he were searching for a rock to throw back.

The old men laughed and snorted through their blackened teeth and filthy beards, exchanging glances as long as there was light. Holme finally told them to be quiet and go to sleep. He listened to the whispering forest for a while through the smoke vent and felt as if he had come home.

In the first gray daylight, a thud woke him up and he opened his eyes to find an ax blade sticking in the wall just above his head. He heard labored breathing, as a pair of hands pulled the ax out and raised it quiveringly again. But it didn't fall a second time.

With a frightened little cry Tan slid back the bar as he saw Stor first in Holme's grip, then slammed to the floor with a crash. He heard an unpleasant cracking, and then he was outside, running toward the forest, then changing direction again for the lake. Halfway down the slope he heard his pursuer's steps behind him and his legs went stiff; he floated as though in a dream. Maybe the water would save him; he had always been the best swimmer at the settlement.

From Holme's silence Tan knew he should expect no mercy. He was old enough to know that a yelling, shouting man wasn't the most dangerous. And he remembered Holme's silent rage from before. He shed his clothes when he reached the landing, ran straight into the water, and started swimming without looking back.

His pursuer didn't rush out into the lake; instead, he returned to the beach and picked up some rocks the size of his fist. The first one flew too far; Tan saw it fall in front of him and turned around. The other fell close in front of him, and when he lifted his hands either to defend himself or ask for mercy the third one hit him right in the head. He saw a brilliant star of sun and water before he sank.

Holme waited a moment but nothing surfaced; the waves rolled peacefully toward the beach as before. When he walked away after a moment, he spied the old men's fishing gear hidden under the logs. It would come in handy. He examined it closely before he returned to the hut.

Stor lay where Holme had left him and would probably never move again. He couldn't take much. Holme dragged him out thinking that if the waves spit Tan onto the shore, the two old men would have each other's company on their journey. They could have lived and lived well if they hadn't tried to ax him in his sleep. In his anxiety, Stor hadn't considered the height of the ceiling. The ax had caromed off the roof and stuck in the wall. Otherwise Holme would be the one lying there now, and the old men would be laughing about their cleverness.

Holme was alone. He went out and sat on a rock on the sunny slope. The wind was wafting over the tall, shimmering grass and he recognized all the smells of summer, from the dry flowers on the slope to the shore's reeds and seaweed. A seabird followed by a column of peeping chicks waddled out of the reeds in exactly the same place where, one summer morning half a lifetime ago, he had emerged from the forest to get weapons for himself and food for Ausi and the newborn baby in the cave.

He let the pigs out, drank water from the spring, and sat down again on the rock. Images from the past meandered across the slope; he saw the chieftain and his family, the buildings, and his fellow thralls. Ausi and he were probably the only ones left alive, now that Stor and Tan were dead.

He felt an intense longing for Ausi and was less angry about her going to the Christians. Someday he would bring her and Tora here; they would rebuild the place and everything would be as before, here where no Christians could lead her astray. They didn't need a wooden god either; he would roll the scorched clump of wood down the slope so it would never bother anyone again.

He heard a powerful snorting from the pigs and saw one of them with its back up standing next to Stor's body. He got up and drove it away thinking that the time had come to dig a grave. Stor lay there, his mouth agape, the wind slowly rustling his beard. His fingers looked as if they were clutching something, although he had dropped the ax when the smith's hands closed around his old body.

The digging was easy between the burial grove and the shore, and there Stor would rest. The next day Holme saw Tan's bumpy back outside the reeds, the waves rocking and washing over him. The anxious thralls, who had been friends their whole lives, had each other's company on the final journey, but they had neither weapons nor provisions. Thralls were used to getting along without either.

They had worried about how the last one of them to die would get buried. They should have been glad they were able to depart and hobble along together wherever they were now.

After visiting a relative's distant farmstead, Geire, Svein, and his mother traveled the same forest road that, a little farther away, led down to the ferry crossing. Geire was thinking of offering his arm and his weapon to some chieftain needing a warrior. Svein and his mother would probably get by in town somehow.

They ran into Tora at a bend in the road, and both parties stopped in surprise. Tora's black eyes passed from one to another, from the woman and the lanky boy, with their hard eyes and faces, to the graying warrior. She looked at him almost with trust and asked to pass by.

The chieftain's wife felt like she recognized the girl but couldn't remember from where. Svein remembered her from the harbor in town, and to him the road, the forest, and everything else immediately lit up, becoming joyful and more pleasant. His only fear was that she would disappear into the forest, never to be seen again.

Geire looked at the girl in wonder too, thinking at first that she was a forest being. The road she was on led into the wasteland, where many things could happen to her. There was something strange about her, and he asked where she was going and why.

She didn't answer his questions, just asked if they had seen her father, the smith. You don't run into many people in the forest; those wandering around in there preferred getting out of each other's way if they were equally matched. If not, the stronger would strike down the weaker and at the very least would rob him of everything he owned. Geire explained all this to the girl and urged her to turn around and return with them before night fell. She was well-dressed, but her face was thin and her bare legs were covered with scratches. Her fingers were stained blue from berries; she must have been on the road for days.

It wasn't until Geire said he was sure her father was already back in town that she turned around and reluctantly followed them. Svein walked sideways the whole time so he could look at her, and his eyes were happy and gentle. But his mother felt a vague dislike for the girl and would have preferred to see her continue into the forest. What did she have to do with them? She with her black eyes and troll-like hair would probably bring them nothing but trouble.

They reached the shore the same evening. The boatman smiled happily when he saw Tora; he said she was like her father, and should have been a boy instead when she ran away. He said too that her mother had come down to look for her every time a boat came in. She was going to be so happy.

There still had been no sign of Holme, but he'd show up. Probably very soon, the boatman said, trying to console Tora when he saw the tears on her cheeks. Clenching her teeth, she said nothing, and she wouldn't look at anyone in the boat.

But the hunger crisis had been averted for the moment; several boats had brought grain and livestock from the other side of the sea. So said the boatman, turning his head to look toward the town. Some figures were standing by the landing, but only a practiced eye could distinguish them from the pilings in the harbor.

Tora sat alone in the prow, and Svein leaned to one side so he could see her from behind the oarsman. It didn't bother him that she didn't look back. He wished there were enemies on the shore so he could show her how he could wield a sword. When he got bigger, he'd search her out and take care of her.

But his mother grimly pondered the memories and feelings the girl had awakened in her. Not even in front of the ashes of her burned home had she felt as strongly about the past as now. With longing and grief she thought of that time when her first husband had been alive, when they had had more than enough warriors and thralls. She had been young and beautiful then, but the long period of thralldom in a foreign land had made her old and ugly.

Among those waiting on the shore, she saw a beautiful middle-aged woman whose troubled face lit up at the sight of the girl in the boat. The bitter woman had a flash of intuition when she saw the familiar shape. The woman had to be the thrall Ausi, who had done her so much harm. The boatman willingly answered her questions and told her that the woman's husband and the girl's father was called Holme and was the best smith in town.

Her first thought was to scream out her discovery and demand justice and revenge. But that would accomplish nothing here where no one knew her or her past. She must wait and consult with Geire. The boatman had spoken in a respectful tone about Holme and his family, and many might be on their side here in town.

Sick with anger, she watched the mother and daughter walk onto a street, but the daughter walked ahead without turning around or acknowledging what her mother said. She seemed like her father even in that regard. All three of them were still her thralls, and when the time was right she would demand to have them back. Or else they'd have to pay a heavy ransom. She was glad they'd brought the girl back with them.

Svein watched Tora for a long time, then slowly followed the same road. From the street corner, he saw the mother vainly try to get her daughter to come into the house. She walked on and the mother followed, crying. Svein smiled to himself, thinking that she was doing the right thing. He could see in her eyes that she was enraged at her mother. Then his own mother called to him, and he fixed in his mind where the girl had gone. He'd come back later and look for her.

Geire was surprised by his sister's impassioned report, impressed that this strange smith, time after time, kept crossing his path. If he was guilty of everything he was accused of, then his end couldn't be far off. Here in town, justice was administered at the assembly, and each accused man had the right to defend himself. The law of the forest was different. However, his sister would go to the assembly to demand her rights. No one had bought the thrall family's freedom; they belonged to her as long as they lived.

They would go to the town's chieftain, lay their case before him, and ask for help. He would surely advise them what to do, and the fugitive thralls would be punished and returned to their owner.

In Holme's smithy, the work went on without him. He had told the smiths more than once that the smithy belonged to all of them. If he or someone else left, the others should carry on. But the work didn't have the same life in it; work would stop for long stretches while the smiths sat talking about everything that had happened and what was likely to come. Holme had fled for his life, but they were sure they'd hear from him somehow. They talked bitterly about Ausi, who had gone back to the Christians again even though they were her husband's enemies. They hoped that Tora had found her father on the mainland; they knew the dangers that awaited a child by herself in the forest.

White eyes and teeth gleamed in the happy blackened faces when Holme's daughter walked into the smithy. All of them liked her although she was generally as quiet and stern as her father. They knew too that, like Holme, she had a good heart and was enraged by injustice and cruelty perpetrated against the defenseless.

She walked in and sat down with them, answering their eager questions with tearful eyes. Ausi stood outside the door, not daring to go in, ignored by them all. With sorrow and bitterness she heard the blackened smiths comforting her daughter, the oldest one stroking her hair, saying she could stay with them until either they heard from Holme or he came back. Ausi felt bitterness again toward Christ, the one who supposedly was the god of love, but who had taken Holme and Tora's love from her. The Christians had promised her that everything would be all right if she was patient and trusted in Christ, but that was a little hard to believe now.

She hesitantly called her daughter's name and was ready to give the Christians up, but no one answered her or came out. She lingered awkwardly there until she heard the bell ringing from the tower. She walked toward it, thinking that Christ still might help if He had a little time. She had given half of all the silver they owned to the church when the Christian priests suggested she should, but things were none the better for it. The other half had to be there when Holme came back.

From the doors of the smithies and the craftsmen's sheds, people watched her, and she could sense that they weren't friendly looks. Everyone knew what had happened and most of them were on Holme's side. Only the rich merchants were partial to Christ and held a grudge against Holme. They secretly considered him just another thrall because he got along so well with them and was always thinking of their welfare.

Ausi was upset by the idleness that had beset her since Holme and Tora had left. The Christians had told her that she should be walking among the heathens, witnessing about Christ and all He could do, but she had refused. Holme would be even more provoked, and she still wasn't so sure that Christ could do so much more than the wooden gods could. If the first stranger who had talked about Christ were still alive, everything would be different. He believed in a different Christ. The summer day she was given to Him at the baptism on the shore was filled with sunshine and promise. But that priest had been tortured to death just like Christ himself. . . .

Suddenly she stopped. Something was lighting up and expanding inside her, and she was breathing heavily. She saw everything now. The stranger had been Christ Himself, come to earth once more. He was as gentle and good as the sun; He tolerated everything without complaint; and He wanted nothing for himself. He endured death without fear. He was Christ, and He had come back for her sake.

She felt her head spin with happiness, and she could clearly see the image of the stranger in front of her after many years of darkness. Next to him, the monks in town now seemed like dark, insignificant human beings. They thought about themselves like everyone else; they calculated and apportioned just like everyone else. They behaved as if Christ were an invisible, powerful wooden god, but she alone knew Him as He was. Only she knew how fine, gentle, and strong He was, both within her and walking beside her. He would take care of everything that troubled her, and she would talk with Him about Holme and Tora.

That was what the stranger had meant when he said that he'd either return or send someone else in his place. And she also knew then why no one had claimed that he was a powerful man in his homeland as people had said about his imitators. He didn't want to be one. She alone knew where he came from and where he had gone.

The two Christian priests stared in surprise at her beaming face as they listened to her story. On the way to the church, she had become more and more convinced that some voice had clarified everything for her, and she told the priests that. But they weren't happy with her; instead, their eyes narrowed and repudiated her. They told her that she had heard the voice of the devil and that she should be on guard. How could a heathen woman like herself presume to think that Christ would reveal Himself to her? The stranger had been sent by the devil to deceive the heathens before Christ's true heralds got there.

But she didn't believe them; they couldn't put out the light she had so recently felt lit inside her. She reminded them of the numerous similarities between Christ and the stranger, of everything they had said about what Christ had experienced and suffered.

Why hadn't any of those who had followed him been sacrificed like him or Christ, she asked, looking at them with penetrating eyes?

But they gave their usual answer that their time hadn't come yet and that Christ alone decided over life and death. That the stranger was killed was his own doing because he was a false teacher, not sent by Christ.

Still Ausi wouldn't give in. Instead she pondered what other evidence there might be for the stranger's being Christ. She remembered what the priests had said about Christ's never having been near a woman. She triumphantly told the men standing before her about the still summer day when the stranger had come to her from town while Holme was away. That her breasts had been exposed, and that she wouldn't have resisted him that warm, lonely day. But he hadn't stayed with her; no one would have stopped him, but he fled from her and disappeared into the forest. Wasn't that doing what Christ Himself would have done?

Again the priests felt her eagerly questioning eyes directed at them. They exchanged looks several times during her story but didn't interrupt her. They realized that the heathens didn't fight very hard against the claims of the flesh if they felt attracted to each other. They understood too that the temptation had been considerable for their unknown predecessor. There was something intensely alluring about the woman before them; she was still in her prime.

In her stubborn, luminous look they saw such a staunch belief in the experience she had imagined that they refrained from admonishing her any further. With time, she'd forget all this and become like the others. The dead monk's words and deeds would fade away before the preaching of the living.

In truth the woman's faith unnerved them, and each secretly wished that his own were as strong and joyous although not as sinful as hers. They told each other that if Christ were to come, she'd open her arms and want to give Him everything. Oblivious of her soul, she would offer Him her body.

And they cursed themselves for the strange feelings these thoughts aroused—a vague jealousy of the stranger who had been sacrificed, but not before carving indelible marks in this beautiful, warm, heathen woman. It was perfectly clear to them that they would never be looked at with such eyes, hers or anyone else's. The heathens who had come to them had other reasons for coming. One was greedy and wondered if Christ could improve his business; another wanted a cure for some disease, refused to believe before he felt completely well, and afterward thought he didn't need any god at all. And they all still secretly worshiped the ancient wooden gods. The moment God's word stopped being preached, it would be forgotten and the wooden gods would reclaim their dark empire. But for years, this woman had carried an image of Christ in her heart, a false image because it hadn't come from them.

When Ausi was taken to the assembly, she thought it was because of what Holme had done. They wanted to find out what she knew and perhaps let her hear him be condemned as an outlaw. She didn't recognize the hard-faced woman standing nearby with a boy and a grizzled warrior.

Without understanding at first what this was all about, Ausi heard parts of her past, from her period of thralldom forward, dragged into the light of day. She saw the warrior pointing at her before he showed the judges that the lanky boy couldn't turn his head. She had seen the boy before and again felt a vague apprehension.

Everything they said was true, and when the gray-haired chieftain who was the judge asked her, she confirmed it. She saw a smug twinkling in the unfamiliar woman's stony face, and then it all became clear to her. They were her old masters intruding into her life again—now when Holme wasn't around to help. Before she fully understood her misfortune, she felt some satisfaction over the chieftain's wife having grown so old and ugly.

The people round about sat listening in silent surprise about her past—the respected smith and his wife were runaway thralls. A number of them nodded their heads, recollecting Holme's always being with the thralls, protecting them. Now they knew why.

Ausi heard herself and Tora condemned to return to their masters and Holme condemned as an outlaw. He wasn't there and they didn't want him back as a thrall. After taxes and other costs had been subtracted, everything they owned would go to the masters—the son and the mother—to compensate for what the masters had lost while the thralls were on the loose for so many years.

She looked around for someone to help, but everyone averted his eyes. The chieftain wouldn't look at her, and the two monks standing nearby conversed quietly and did nothing for her. After the judgment had fallen, the old chieftain's wife came up and, hissing a few words dripping with hate, grabbed Ausi violently by the arm. There was nothing but silence as she was dragged off to be a thrall in her own house.

The two women, Geire, and Svein, walked between the heathen temple and the Christian church, but everything was quiet and still there too. The church was closed, but in the door of the shrine she saw the wooden god stare rigidly at her. Neither Christ nor the wooden god wanted to help her. Only Holme would, the one she had harmed, but he was far away and knew nothing about this.

The chieftain's wife looked Holme's house over with satisfaction and decided where everyone's place would be. Geire's cheekbones were red under his beard, and he mumbled that he'd be on his way soon. He wanted neither to have any part of the thralls' possessions nor to live in their house. All he had wanted was justice for his sister. Svein too looked angrily at his mother and wouldn't respond to her words, tender though they became whenever she turned to him.

Ausi took her place by the door, once the keys to the lock Holme had forged were taken from her. The chieftain's wife rifled greedily through the family's possessions—clothes, jewelry, and ornaments that Holme had made or bartered for. She let the silver nuggets and foreign coins run between her fingers while Geire, clearing his throat in disgust, got up and left. Svein was keenly interested in some swords and spears of unusual shape hanging on the low wall above the master's place.

Then came Ausi's turn. Her mistress took her own raggedy clothes off and ordered Ausi to trade with her. Ausi obeyed, thinking that her years as a respected and free housewife had been just a dream. Everything was as before—worse than before—without Holme, Tora, and her thrall companions.

Ausi's newfound joy couldn't fully compensate for what had befallen her that day, but as she lay on the floor listening to the other three breathing quietly on the sleeping benches, some of it returned. When her lot was this hard, she was almost like Christ and the stranger. They would probably notice and send help. He would come Himself or send someone in His place, but not one of the priests. The best thing would be if He found Holme and let him know how things stood. Happily she imagined how terrified her owner, Geire, and the boy would be if Holme suddenly appeared in the doorway, huge, silent, and deadly. No judges or swords would help them then.

She also found it strange that neither Christ nor the wooden gods had destroyed Holme, since he had despised and persecuted both them and their servants. Could it be that they liked Holme despite all that, just as the most powerful warriors did, eyeing him with a certain respect, not daring to treat him as they did the other thralls? That was probably the case, and it was to the benefit of all three of them—Holme, Ausi, and Tora.

Perhaps things were not as the priests had told her. They could have misunderstood things despite their being priests. Christ really should go straight to Holme and talk with him frankly, man to man. No crying, ringing bells, or sacrifices. They could be friends, and with Holme on his side, Christ could feel secure about His church and followers.

The chieftain's wife had locked up all the weapons and had gone to sleep with the keys still on her. She was probably afraid that Ausi would try to kill them in their sleep. But it would be better if Ausi herself were dead and gone. As long as she, Holme, or Tora were alive, their old masters would hate them and hurt them whenever they could. The woman had growled at Ausi that the settlement had been ravaged and burned by thieves, she'd been taken into thralldom in a foreign land, and had recently been saved by a raid there. She said further that Holme's evil power had been the cause of all that misfortune. But Holme had no evil power, he who was so good to all thralls and all the oppressed.

Ausi was also thinking that there was an end now to her going to the Christian buildings and yard for the worship services. That didn't feel so bad now that she knew more about Christ than the monks did. He would come straight to her once more, but this time she'd be able to recognize Him and not look at Him as she would an ordinary man. Then He'd hear all about her, Holme, and Tora. She wouldn't even keep quiet about the thing called sin. He'd listen with the gentle smile she remembered so well and then destroy all their enemies and reunite her with Holme and Tora. Later on, when they had been dead and buried for a while, He would raise all three of them and ascend with them into heaven.

In her heart, she was thankful that Holme hadn't been at the assembly. Many would have fallen before his rage, but in the end, he would have fallen before the swords of the many warriors. The chieftain's wife would have been even happier if she could have seen him dead. She couldn't really feel safe from him now; she spent the whole first day in his house listening and trembling whenever anyone passed by outside. You could also hear in her voice that she was uneasy, even though several times she assured them that he had received his just punishment and was no longer walking among the living.

But Ausi paid no attention to her; she knew Holme was alive and would come back. She felt it in her heart and so could endure her new thralldom. With Christ and Holme living peacefully together within her, who could do her harm?

She could hear the wind outside among the buildings, moving heavily the way it did just before a rain. A cold draft blew in under the door, and once a pig came right up to it, rooting and snorting. She was in an uncomfortable position and had to turn over, but maybe Holme had it even worse. Christ, of course, had once had to sleep with a stone or a clump of grass for a pillow. And she was weaker and more sinful than He or Holme; why should she have it any better?

But Holme wouldn't be very nice when he learned that Ausi was sleeping as a thrall by her own door.

She had been without a man for many days now and was feeling an unquenchable longing. Finally she fell asleep, imagining alternately her dark-complected Holme and the light-complected stranger next to her breast. After a while Geire woke up, raised his head, and listened to her regular breathing. Then he looked toward his sister's bed, sighed, and laid his head down again. For a long time, he visualized the thrall's beautiful face and ripe body. But she wouldn't be receptive to him because he had done her harm. Besides, she was the kind who'd only give herself to the man who had claimed her heart.

A couple of days later one of the Christian priests came to her. He told her solemnly that what had happened was punishment for her grave sin of calling a false teacher, sent by the devil, Christ. She should bear her punishment with humility and gratitude because it came at such an early stage of the sin. That was a sign that she hadn't been cast away from the face of God for eternity.

But something inside Ausi told her that his words were empty and that he was talking about some other Christ. The real one would come to her, not send someone like him. She felt almost happy when the chieftain's wife interrupted the priest and started loudly telling the story of all the evil Holme and his family had inflicted upon her.

Svein wandered down among the smithies looking for Tora. He had seen her go that way and thought she might still be there. He finally caught a glimpse of her walking into the biggest smithy, a wooden bucket in hand. Soon afterward the sledgehammers stopped clanging.

Svein sneaked up to the door and looked in. A number of big smiths were sitting around a table eating. Tora was standing by the hearth looking into the fire, blowing on it occasionally with a hand bellows. Before he knew it, Svein was standing there inside the smithy, all the smiths' eyes directed at him.

The judgment against Ausi was already known throughout the

town, but even if the smiths thought she deserved it, they couldn't stand Holme's former owner moving into his house and taking everything he owned. They laughed scornfully at Svein's message that the daughter should join her mother to begin her thralldom. No one would lay a hand on her as long as the smiths could lift a hammer or an ax.

They recognized the stiff-necked youth and looked at him in surprise. How did he dare come here? He paid them no heed but instead stared at Tora, his blue eyes twinkling with admiration. The smiths stopped eating, waiting to see what was going to happen.

When Tora first caught sight of him, she looked away immediately, her mouth drawing into a scornful smile. Then she dropped the bellows, picked up a handful of soot, and walked up to the boy who was standing there motionless, following her with his eyes. He didn't even try to protect himself when she threw the soot in his face; he just kept staring at her as if he were under a spell.

The smiths' roaring laughter brought him out of it, and he wiped the soot from his eyes. He looked at his dirty hand, and his face became hard and angry. He took a step or two toward Tora, who had returned to the fire pit, but one of the smiths stuck his foot out, and Svein fell flat on his face on the black floor. When he came to again, he was lying outside the smithy with a sooty and bloody face.

Sobbing with rage, he got up and shook his fists defiantly at the smiths even though he felt great fear of their strength. When he grew up, he'd come back and take the girl by force if she wouldn't come of her own free will. He had a right to her; she belonged to him and his mother.

Ausi was pleased when he came home and his mother pried out

of him how he had been treated at the smithy. She remembered the uneasiness she had felt when she had seen the stiff-necked boy a number of years ago. Now she was glad that Tora had mighty defenders when she herself was powerless and Holme was gone. Holme could take credit for this; without the respect and friendship the smiths felt for him, they wouldn't have cared what happened to his daughter.

But Ausi's owner could see she was gloating. She yanked her by the hair and listed the things she'd do to Tora once she had her in her clutches. Next year they would go back and rebuild the settlement; her son would be the chieftain and the thralls would be closely watched so they couldn't escape to pretend they were freemen and as good as their masters.

Ausi was thinking, however, that Holme would soon come to her rescue and avenge all these wrongs. Christ would give him the message soon. As she watched her owner pluck her blond hair from her fingers, she fantasized about the moment when Holme would appear in the door. Everything would change in that instant and peaceful, happy years would return. Holme and Tora would learn to know the real Christ and they wouldn't scorn Him because He was as good and true as they were.

She hoped Holme wouldn't take long. There was a great deal of malice in the mother's and son's eyes and it was flashing at her and Tora.

A number of starving vagabonds had come to Holme during the winter and spring; he had given them what he could and seen them on their way. A couple had stayed for a few days to help with the construction, and a younger woman had chosen not to go on but instead had stayed and shared his bed until a man came and got her. The man wasn't angry; he talked calmly with Holme about the woman. He hadn't been able to keep her from leaving when there was no more food in his house. But things were better now, and he had searched the area for her for a long time. He said too that if he had found another woman, Holme could have kept the first one.

But Holme let them go their way and was relieved when they disappeared down the path. The woman looked back frequently, crying into her arm. She had worked hard and willingly, perhaps believing it was for her own benefit. Her husband was no bigger than she was and had a scraggly beard. There weren't many women around; that's why he had traveled so far looking for her. He had gotten her back in more supple and beautiful condition than when she had left. Holme thought as he watched them go that if she had gone to any man other than himself, the two men would have had to fight over her.

That evening he paced restlessly around the empty house. He missed the woman's shy smile when he came in the door, and now and then he wished he had held onto her.

He had doubled the size of his house and had weatherproofed it with mud. He had also sown larger areas than the thralls had, thinking that there should be grain enough for several during the winter. Before the woman had shown up, his longing for Ausi and Tora had been so great that he had geared up to return but had controlled himself because everything had to be ready first. They would buy cows, pigs, and iron for tools with the silver in the chest.

One day, when the golden grain was swaying on the slope, he saw a small boat approaching shore. He walked down the path, ax in hand, and the man in the boat rested hesitantly on his oars a little way out. Then he let out a surprised yell and rowed eagerly in. He called Holme by name and ran up to him, his face glowing with happiness.

It was one of the starving thralls from town who had helped divide up the Christian grain. Holme couldn't quite recognize the emaciated man but was glad that he might get some news about his family now anyway. The thrall hadn't been on his journey for very many days. He immediately told Holme how he had taken the boat from a farmstead where, rather than giving him something to eat, they had set dogs on him.

He ate the whole time he talked. Holme was relieved his daughter was in good hands, but when the thrall told about Ausi's new enslavement, he got up and walked to the door so the thrall couldn't see his face. When he turned around again, he began taking stock of weapons, and the thrall got uneasy at the signs of imminent departure. He certainly would have preferred to stay there where there was both food and safety.

The thrall talked on about how peaceful the town had been during the winter and spring once the king had sent grain and meat. But the black blight had come back again on the wind and settled on the ripening barley. It had to be the fertility god who had sent this misfortune, and everywhere people were beginning to see that he must be appeased if they didn't want famine to ravage the entire land.

The thrall also told Holme that the Christians had gained many followers among the wealthy merchants. But everyone else, craftsmen and thralls, were convinced that the Christians were responsible for the blight. If they were killed or driven off, the blight would vanish with them and everything would be like it was before. But the monks were under the king's protection, and no one dared lift a hand against them.

Holme said nothing, but when his weapons were ready, he found an ax and spear for the thrall. He hid the leftover grain and let the pigs out. The two men walked around, carefully examining the grain swaying and whispering in the wind, but there was no sign of blight. The thrall looked at the crude god on the stone and said he'd guard the grain and everything else at the settlement. No Christians were provoking him out here in the woods.

They left the next morning after Holme refused to let the thrall stay and keep an eye on things until Holme could return with his family. Deep behind the thrall's bushy eyebrows, Holme sensed a hope lurking that Holme would not come back at all. He knew that Holme's life was worthless among the freemen, and he could be the new owner of this beautiful and peaceful place beyond the forests. Going to town could mean his life too.

But Holme was adamant, causing the thrall to fall silent and give up the hope that had momentarily sprung up. Like most people, he felt a fear inside that Holme could do more than other men. It was rumored that no weapon could harm him. But he could kill a man with nothing but his bare hands.

Thin and scraggly, the thrall plodded along through the marshy ground, over the ridge by the cave, and then up to the pathless woods. Silent and huge, Holme walked beside him, answering his ingratiating words with a grumble. They walked toward town and perhaps toward death.

The last night Geire spent in Holme's house, he could no longer restrain his craving for the thrall woman lying on the floor by the door. Day after day he had watched her tantalizing face and gentle movements and couldn't get her out of his mind. He thought about how long it had been since he had had a woman and now he was leaving on another long journey.

He listened to her even breathing, thinking that if he sneaked up on her, she couldn't wake up to defend herself until it was too late. His sister was sleeping too, and if she woke up it would be awkward, but not dangerous. She wouldn't say a word about it.

He hesitated a long time, but the night was drawing to a close. Through the vent in the ceiling he had just heard the town guard challenge an early visitor. He himself would be gone soon after the sun came up.

Ausi was asleep and unaware when the bearded warrior sat down on the floor beside her. She was lying on her side and had her garment on top of her like a blanket. For a moment Geire thought this act was beneath him, but through the darkness he saw a bare white shoulder and couldn't force himself to get up again.

He had imagined her sleeping on her back; now she might wake up too quickly and be harder to handle. He slowly put his hand on her hip and carefully pushed her over on her back. Her breathing stopped for a moment, and he thought she'd wake up. But then she turned her head to the side and slept more deeply in her new position. Geire carefully pulled the clothes away from her, the clasps softly jingling. Someone was walking by outside, although it was still night. The footsteps stopped and Geire hesitated, waiting until he heard them continue down the street.

It had never been any use for a thrall woman to scream for help when a man took her, but Ausi fought with silent fury. She couldn't throw the weight off her, but she could heave it back and forth. Panting heavily, the warrior grumbled in bitter disappointment.

The struggle woke the chieftain's wife, and when it became clear to her what was happening, she whispered an angry order in the midst of everything for Ausi to stop resisting. As the woman drew closer, Ausi could hear her whispering harsh, scornful words that she should be glad to have a man other than her black-haired thrall. The warrior said nothing, but Ausi could feel his coarse beard on her neck, and he was panting more and more heavily. On the other hand, she still had some strength left and began to hope she might save herself.

But then she felt a pair of hard hands on her arms; they yanked her hands back, away from the rapist's chest, so she couldn't fend him off any longer. Her arms were pulled back over her head and pinned to the floor by the chieftain's wife, who kept hissing insults. The warrior finally vanquished her weakening legs, and the battle was over. The sky had begun to turn gray through the smoke vent, and the table and benches emerged from the darkness. On one of them lay Svein; his eyes were closed and he was breathing deeply.

When the struggle on the floor had awakened the chieftain's wife and she saw Geire's empty bed, she was angry that he had lowered himself to seek the loathsome thrall. But when she heard the fierce resistance and realized that Ausi was doing all she could to get free, she quickly changed her mind. Did that thrall still dare oppose her masters?

And when Geire and she together had subdued the thrall, she had gleefully listened to Ausi's sobbing, rhythmically broken by the man's thrusts. She felt Ausi's arms relax, and when the man got up, averting his face, Ausi had turned toward the door and lain still. The chieftain's wife whispered a few scornful remarks and returned to her bed, but Geire put on his clothes in the first light of day shining through the smoke vent. After getting his weapons, he walked to the door and pulled back the bar, stepped over Ausi, and disappeared.

Svein had awakened because something in the room was moving. He sensed immediately that it had nothing to do with him, but a curious excitement took hold of him, sending warm waves through his body. He looked toward the two figures he could hear breathing on the floor and listened excitedly.

He could make out something white emerging from the darkness, and for an instant he could see the entire female body. Then it was hidden by something dark and the fight began. He heard his mother wake up and join in and he sat up on his bed to see better. He could see the white legs flailing and hands grabbing at them to hold them still. All three were panting and no one noticed him. When the battle was over and only weak sounds could be heard, he sank back on his bed, terrified by the new things he felt inside. It wasn't what had happened on the floor that had kindled the fire within him—he had imagined himself and the woman's daughter in the same position. That's how it should be someday, otherwise he didn't want to go on living. Instantly he thought that it was shameful for such old people to do what they had done—that belonged to the young. He didn't want to look at them, so he shut his eyes and kept breathing deeply when they got up. But it would be fun to see how the thrall looked—to see if she had been changed much by all this. Geire left and that was for the best; he didn't want to look at him anymore.

But now he and his mother had to find a way to get the girl. She belonged to them, and he yearned for her so much his whole body ached. His mother had always tried to get him whatever he wanted; and he wanted the girl from the smithy.

Several farmsteads lined the road leading out of the forest toward town. Once they had housed large herds of animals, but now there were only solitary cows or pigs. Most of the animals had died during the year of famine.

The grain fields were swaying in the warm breeze, but the thrall triumphantly showed Holme that the black blight, which had come on the wind, was clinging to the ears. It had consumed the insides so that the empty ears rattled delicately. A dour man there predicted that those who survived the winter wouldn't see another summer since there were no animals for them. He shook his fist at the town and cursed the Christians. Then he took Holme and the thrall to a stone, full of small hollows, to show them he had never stopped smearing those hollows with fat. But the fertility god must be angrier than ever before; nothing seemed to help.

He offered them some of his bread, light and dry with bran, but they had their own provisions. When he heard that they were going to town and were embittered about the Christians, he picked up his weapons to go along. His wife and child looked mutely at him when he turned around to tell them what they ought to do while he was gone.

Holme was thinking that what he wanted to do in town he would do alone as always, but he couldn't keep anyone else from going there. There was no grain to gather, no animals to tend; there was nothing else for a farmer to do than take his weapons from the wall.

The new man asked them to take a detour with him to his relatives' farmstead. It was a day's journey, and there they found three grim men and blight on the grain. Then there were six men walking toward town, and the group increased little by little. They all considered Holme the leader although no one had chosen him and he didn't say much himself. Several knew him from town, and a few had bartered with him.

Before dawn of the third day, the group was standing on the shore, and the oarsman, who had been sleeping in the boat, stared at them in consternation. If all of them wanted to go across, he'd be rowing all morning. But there were several boats by the shore, and most of them would have to row themselves across. He didn't often see so many silent, well-armed men showing up at once during peacetime.

When he caught sight of Holme and noticed that all the others turned to him, he knew that danger was in the offing and he'd have to proceed cautiously when he reached town with the first group.

Holme was among those taking a seat in his boat; the rest manned the other boats and followed them. In the middle of the lake, the oarsman was ordered to change course to the shore west of town. He was thinking that when they reached shore he'd run to town with the news. They wouldn't be able to catch him in the short stretch to the nearest town gate.

But that changed too. Holme said a few words and the oarsman found himself surrounded by stern men while the boat was rowed back to fetch those on the opposite shore. Holme himself disappeared into the darkness toward town. The guard at the gate peered sleepily and disagreeably at him but didn't stop him from passing through.

Holme walked past his house and listened for a moment. Inside a man sat on the floor beside the sleeping Ausi, listening to the steps outside. Had Holme returned a short time later, he would have heard the panting and struggling that began on the other side of the door as soon as his steps had died away. Then many things would have been different for many people.

The smithies were silent but he greedily breathed in the smell of soot and iron. He walked to the oldest smith's house and knocked on the door. It took a while for the smith to appear, ax in hand. He immediately recognized the massive figure standing in the darkness and let out a happy yell, put his ax down and opened the door wide.

Holme looked around eagerly when he entered, and with a smile the smith laid a few sticks on the fire so that it came to life. Tora was sleeping on a bench, and her father sat beside her, watching her silently. A moment later the smith saw Holme's cheeks glisten with moisture he brushed off on the sleeve of his shirt. Then Holme softly told the smith what was going on and asked him to wake the others.

While Holme waited and the smith's wife busied herself by the fire, Tora woke up and saw her father in the firelight. However, she had seen the vision in her dreams several times, and so was afraid to move. But then he turned toward her, and the two pairs of dark eyes met. She leaped up with a scream and threw her arms around his neck. She clung to him, just as she had as a child when he had found her in the garbage pile with the dogs and pigs. Her eyes twinkled with joy and pride as she looked at her father and complained about how the Christians had treated her. Neither of them mentioned Ausi.

Holme sent the smiths all over town to call thralls and craftsmen together who wanted to join them. It would be daylight soon, and before then they had to assemble so quietly and inconspicuously that no one sounded the alarm or closed the gates. Holme went back to the shore with the smith and Tora.

The last of the boats were out on the lake, and the shore was swarming with men. When they were all there, they discussed what to do, and it was decided that the guards at the gate would have to be struck down if they wouldn't take their side against the Christians.

Dawn was just beginning to break when the group approached the rampart near the shore. Men kept coming, wild, emaciated men in rags who had been sleeping in the surrounding areas—

thralls who had been driven off when the famine came. They crowded happily around Holme, and his face softened for an instant.

The guard saw a couple of men approaching and took a position by the bar to get a better look at them. He had no idea that long files of additional men were sneaking along the rampart. When he challenged those directly in front of him, he found himself surrounded by silent, armed men who immediately disarmed him. But the other guard ran along the rampart gangway, yelling for someone to sound the alarm.

Meanwhile, the intruders kept heading toward the smithies. Many windows opened up a crack, and surprised faces peeked out as they passed. Such a strange troop had never moved through the town at that time of the day before. Heading the group was the huge master smith and his daughter, followed by many nameless, well-armed men, and finally by ragged, emaciated thralls armed with clubs and axes. Many of the townspeople began gathering the things together they'd need when they fled to the fortress, although no alarm had been sounded and no order had come from the chieftain.

But people were hurrying toward the smithies from everywhere, and when some of them met some others, they'd talk in low, excited voices, then join the others. A message was sent to the heathen priest across from the Christian church to light the sacrificial fire at once. The underside of a long cloud bank in the east gradually reddened—the time was near.

In the smithies, the thralls were handing out axes and spears, and rage and greed flashed from their eyes. The farmers watched them calmly and without disdain; working in the fields, on the lake, and in the forest had brought lord and thrall closer together than they could ever be with merchants and townspeople. The farmers wanted to strike down the enemy so that the fertility god would look on them again with favor, and then they wanted to go home. But the thralls were fighting for something to eat, for revenge for countless wrongs, and because they were miserable. Holme wanted to fight because he recognized the great injustice and abuse looming over anyone held in servitude.

Meanwhile, Holme was getting uneasy about what to do with all these men once their job was done. The farmers would surely return to their farmsteads, believing that there would then be a good crop free of blight, but there were dozens of thralls. It would be just like the year before when they were starving and homeless, following him like dogs, waiting silently for him to do whatever he could do for them. But he couldn't do anything, and many of them would go back to their owners, if they survived the famine, and be whipped or even killed; others would disappear in the forests. Their skulls and bones would lie there turning white in the moss under some branch.

Then a thought hit him like a punch. They'd all do as he had— go back to the mainland and live on their own. He had broken free of thralldom; why couldn't they all do that? Land was everywhere, even some burned out, abandoned farmsteads where the fields were still in good shape. They could take thrall women with them as wives or get them later. But no one who had once been a thrall would ever have a thrall himself.

Holme was very happy about all this; it seemed so simple and right. All the thralls could walk the same road he had walked to freedom. Many of them were too feeble to make their way themselves, but the others could lend them a hand.

His chest expanded as he envisioned a land and people free of masters and thralls. Everyone was happy there, no one had to fight for his possessions or his life. The vision clouded over and disappeared, but he never forgot it. The thralls, who were brandishing their axes, clubs, and spears in the air around him as they were waiting to leave, saw his face soften toward them, but didn't know why.

He had no plan in mind when they marched up toward the Christian buildings and yard; he was used to letting the moment dictate its own terms. The merchants and maybe the town guard from the fortress would stand against them and the battle might be hard. When it was over, he would show the thralls the land he had just seen; then they'd fight to attain it even if he were gone.

From the chieftain's buildings and yard, the Christians saw the smoke billowing from the heathen shrine early that morning. Shortly, there was a loud knock on the door, and anxious men told them that Holme had come back with armed men to throw the town into chaos. Everything had been so peaceful and had gone so well for the Christians during the year he had been away.

But the chieftain wasn't concerned that some masterless thralls had gathered together at the smithies. Starved as they were, they'd be quickly defeated. Little unpleasantries like this came with hard times. But their leader would be captured and punished because he had dared come back to town. He would have been better off if he had never shown his face again. He always had been a trouble-maker, unlike the others, both masters and thralls.

The rumor spread quickly in the early morning, and many people closed up their houses and sought protection with the chieftain. Among them were Ausi's mistress and her son, and they took their thrall along so she wouldn't escape. Ausi wasn't aware yet that Holme had returned, but she had already decided to run away and find Holme on the mainland, even if she got lost on the way. She kept imagining the stranger there with her, Christ there with her, and kept asking Him for help. The outrage perpetrated on her was now affecting her innermost being; for a long time she had belonged only to Holme and Christ, although He didn't care about women in that way.

But the chieftain's wife gave her no opportunity to escape. She was carefully guarded on the way. The streets were almost deserted, but from the smithies you could hear muffled voices and activity. A skinny, ragged thrall, his eyes glistening, came running toward them, rushed by, and kept going down toward the smithies. In front of them a richly clad merchant's family was hurrying toward the Christian yard.

When the chieftain's scout returned and told him how many thralls, farmers, and craftsmen were gathered together at the smithies, the chieftain sent a message to the town guard inside the fortress. They were powerful, seasoned warriors, and their presence would terrify the pack of thralls into submission or flight. It would never have to come to a fight.

The Christians were called together by ringing the bell, and a fisherman, out on the lake, rested on his oars, looking toward town as the peal rolled out over the reeds and water. He had never heard the Christian bells so early before. A ship was getting ready to leave the harbor, but that was all the life he saw. Maybe the priests were sailing home on it and were being honored by the bells.

The monotonous ringing was also a signal to Holme and his band. Several of the mainland farmers listened in surprise to the strange sound they were hearing for the first time. A couple of thralls had found some big horns, which they wanted to try out. They looked each other in the eye, puffed out their cheeks, and played a tune they usually called each other with in the forests. Between the shrill blasts on the horn, the Christian bells tinkled out full, but thin, notes.

Holme had never imagined he'd return like this. He had thought he'd be alone as always when he had his showdown with his enemies. But when this band with him realized they'd have to drive out the Christians in order to survive, you couldn't stop them. In the end, they'd probably be condemned as outlaws, but the forests on the mainland were large and could protect as many as poured into them.

The horn blasts, when they rose shrill from the woods, answering each other morning and evening, made him recall his days as a thrall. It was the song of the thralls, and so he let the two with the horns take the lead to the Christian yard. Over and over again, they sounded the song of the forest, used to call for help when wild animals attacked their cows or pigs.

The chieftain, the Christian priests, and a group of armed merchants were standing outside the Christian yard when the blaring horns approached from the side street, drowning out the bells. They saw Holme's band swarming, crowding together in front of the shrine of the wooden god, where the sacrificial smoke was constantly billowing, and where the smell of burnt flesh hung above the courtyard. The open area between the shrine and the church soon filled, and the thralls lowered the horns, panting from the strain of blowing them. At the same time the bells also stopped— the large one with a tentative, final clang—and all was quiet. Only the murmuring of praying voices inside the Christian church blended with the crackling of the heathen sacrificial fire.

For a moment, Holme had doubts about what to do. He had never been able to attack before he had been provoked. Nor could he assail with words. But from the silence behind him, one of the farmers from the blighted farmsteads came forward. He had talked at the assembly before, and he began speaking in a relaxed but powerful voice.

He leveled sharp words at the chieftain, who was clinging to the Christians and protecting them. The Christians and their followers had brought calamity on the land and the people by angering the ancient gods. For the second year, the blight had ravished the entire land, and it was being said everywhere that the Christians were at fault. They insisted that the Christians return to their homeland before something worse happened, and that their temple be torn down. Otherwise it would come to a fight and the farmers might just as well die that way as return to their farmsteads and starve to death with their families.

When the farmer had finished, the others demonstrated that he had spoken for them. Those with shields beat on them, as they would at the assembly; the others shouted and roared. The thralls stood silent, feeling as usual that no one had spoken for them. They all knew that Holme spoke best with his sledgehammer and fists.

When it grew quiet again, the chieftain came forward to show he wasn't afraid of them. In an angry voice he called them foolish heathens and ordered each and every one of them to go home. He would, however, answer the farmers' charges if the thralls were driven away and Holme was captured. How could freemen from the mainland allow themselves to be led by an outlaw and runaway thrall, he scornfully asked.

It was apparent that he had said the right things. The farmers seemed to wake up and look at each other and the thralls solemnly and awkwardly. They had always thought the smith was a respected man; they knew nothing about his thralldom or his guilt. They had seen the noblest people in town doing business in Holme's smithy.

Holme sensed their hesitation and mounting disdain, and he felt a sense of relief. He hadn't known how he would relate to them. They had farmsteads and land; he couldn't plead their case. They were no part of him or the thralls. If they pulled out now, his hands would be free. Then it only concerned him and the thralls, and no one would even talk to the thralls.

Just as before, not knowing what he should do made Holme furious. The thralls stood close behind him waiting for a word or action from him. The farmers were standing to one side, conferring among themselves. The chieftain turned directly to him, scornfully ordering him to give himself up and the thralls to disperse and return to their masters.

Holme felt his hesitation transform into a rage, which flowed out into his arms. His sledgehammer rose up and fell with a mighty blow against the nearest leg of the bell tower. It snapped like a straw and the bells groaned, but the tower remained standing on its two other legs. Then the sledgehammer fell again, and the tower teetered to one side while the chieftain and those close by leaped out of the way. It quickly toppled over and the bells hit the ground with a muffled clang. The thralls laughed and began hacking wildly with their axes at the prostrate tower.

At the chieftain's signal, some Christian warriors advanced toward the thralls but soon had to retreat before the dense, wild group of axes, clubs, and spears. Seeing this, the chieftain gave a new order for someone to get the warriors who hadn't arrived yet from the fortress. The Christian priests hurried into the temple, followed by women and children; the doors were shut and the bar thrown before the thralls could stop it. While some of them followed the retreating warriors, deriding them, Holme's sledgehammer resounded against the church door and soon smashed it to bits. The thralls pressed in after him and the heathen priests urged them on with loud yells from the shrine.

One of the Christian priests headed straight down the aisle for Holme, carrying a cross in front of him while he called on his god in a loud voice. He barred the way, and Holme lowered his sledge-hammer before the unarmed man. But one of the thralls stepped forward and hacked the priest down with his ax. He fell in the aisle, his cross beneath him, gasped a few more words to his god, and then lay still.[10]

When the other priest saw that their lives were in danger, he opened a small door behind the altar and let the terrified women and children crawl out. He waited until last, and no one cut him down, although he witnessed the thralls' axes smash savagely into the benches and Holme's sledgehammer fall on the altar with a deafening crash. The holy relics bounced high into the air and landed in the hands of thralls, who fondled them curiously. Then they were on top of him, the point of a spear thrusting through the door as he made his escape.

After the thralls had demolished everything in the church, they gathered again in the open area outside the shrine. It was almost deserted; most of the Christians had run for shelter with the chieftain. The farmers stood to the side, ignoring the victorious thralls'

10. Rimbert reports Nithard's death as follows: "It happened, too, at this time, at the instigation of the devil, that the Swedish people were inflamed with zeal and fury, and began by insidious means to persecute Bishop Gautbert. Thus it came about that some of the people, moved by a common impulse, made a sudden attack upon the house in which he was staying, with the object of destroying it; and in their hatred of the Christian name they killed Nithard, and made him, in our opinion, a true martyr" (*Anskar,* chapter 17, p. 59). The second revolt led by Holme, then, has some historical validity, although Rimbert does not mention thralls or hunger as a motivating force. The revolt of the previous year, however, is Fridegård's fabrication.

taunting yells. The warriors from the fortress came at a run, and the chieftain opened the gate as they approached. There weren't as many of them as there were thralls, but they were well-armed, seasoned men.

The chieftain talked with them a moment and pointed toward the band of thralls. The warriors turned around and looked at the emaciated, wild throng that stood mutely waiting. First was Holme; they knew him well and respected him for his strength and skill. Around him were the other smiths, who were nothing to play with, then the dense ranks of thralls, starving and mistreated. They would fight like wolves because they had nothing to lose and everything to gain. They were leaning on their axes, spears, and sledgehammers. The whole dismal band awaited the attack and wouldn't be scared off. If it came to a fight, it would cost many warriors their lives.

Many of the warriors secretly approved what had just happened at the Christian yard. They would gladly see Christ and his servants driven off or killed so that all would be as before. Holme and his men had done a good deed and the wooden gods would approve it.

The highest-ranking warrior spoke with the chieftain and said that it was their duty to defend the town against foreign invaders, but they would have nothing to do with what they saw standing before them. Why had the thralls been allowed through the gates and given the chance to arm themselves? And they hadn't attacked the town or anything attached to it, just the temple of the foreigners. The shrine stood there untouched. They would answer to the king for refusing to attack the thralls and craftsmen.

Meanwhile, everyone who had run for cover with the chieftain came out into the open again. A few of them picked up the dead

Christian priest and carried him across the open area while the surviving monk followed along with head bowed. The chieftain's wife was at the front, her eyes full of hatred for Holme. She had expected to see him captured and cut down and couldn't understand why he was still standing there like a free and significant man. Svein stared at him too, unable to control a shudder before the figure of terror from his childhood. Ausi and the other thrall women were locked in a room so they couldn't join their husbands and brothers among the thralls.

For the second time, the chieftain ordered his warriors to clear the thralls from the building, but they pretended not to hear and assumed indifferent expressions. They looked around, yawned hugely, and talked softly among themselves. The sun was high over the lake, and the two bells lying in the grass between the two groups of people glistened in the sunlight. The heathen priests had moved the wooden god forward, and he stood, freshly smeared with blood, looking out over the open area with his angular face. But the Christian church was empty and gutted, and Christ hadn't struck down any of His enemies.[11] The warriors couldn't hide their delight over all that had happened without their help.

Rumor of the disturbance soon reached the harbor, and the ship that Geire had already boarded postponed its departure. Many of the warriors on board had relatives in town and didn't want to leave until they knew the final outcome.

Geire passed by Holme's closed house and walked toward the Christian buildings and yard. Everywhere he saw people going in

11. Contrary to Fridegård's account, Rimbert tells us that almost all involved in the attack on the Christians were soon punished (*Anskar*, chapter 18, p. 59).

the same direction, many of them carrying their valuables. In the distance, he could see the warriors racing down the slope by the fortress, fixing their clothes and weapons as they went. Something serious must have happened.

He was glad to see Holme at the head of the thralls. He wouldn't escape his punishment this time, and Geire's sister would finally be avenged. He stood listening to the exchange between the chieftain and the leader of the warriors and became afraid that the dangerous smith would get away. He walked up to the chieftain, explained briefly what had happened at his sister's farmstead, and asked if he could take revenge on Holme. He shrugged his shoulders at the warnings that came from several directions around him. But the chieftain was glad for this solution—no one would deny an unimpeachable warrior his right to cut down an outlaw.

Geire took an ax and walked across the open area as if he were going to chop down a dry tree. He drew his sword only against his equals. But he had forgotten that for thralls there were no rules of battle. They sensed what he wanted, and his disdainful bearing angered them. A threatening murmur rose from their ranks. The thralls knew that without Holme they were lost, and this warrior was coming at him with an ax. They forced their way past Holme, and Geire soon found himself surrounded. Hard, emaciated faces were all around him and he begrudgingly looked for help. But the warriors stood by indifferently, and the chieftain's threatening shout had no effect.

Geire raised his ax but it never touched a single thrall. A club struck him from behind, knocking him to the ground. A woman screamed shrilly, following that with a flood of insults for men who didn't dare take on thralls. Holme recognized the voice and then the woman with her hard face. She was the one who had forced Ausi back into thralldom.

Through the brief silence that descended once Geire had been struck down came another shout, a woman's voice, distant but still strangely near. There was both hope and despair in the shout.

"Holme!"

The shout sounded twice, and the second time Holme distinctly heard it come from a small building at the back of the chieftain's property. Those standing closest to Holme got out of the way before he had even moved, and many scurried toward the doors to seek shelter from the silent smith, whom they had seen in their town for so many peaceful years. A path opened before him as he rushed toward the building, and the thralls clamored after him, trampling Geire under their bare feet.

But Holme didn't touch anyone fleeing from him, paying no attention to friend or foe. When he got to the building, he heard the shout once more, weaker this time, as if someone were trying to force Ausi to shut up. There was no back door and the front door was already barred from the inside. He was aware that the warriors had left the open area, but the farmers were still there, uncertain what to do.

For a moment Holme hesitated to smash open a building that belonged to the chieftain. But it was his woman who was screaming, and he wasn't concerned anymore about her having gone to the Christians. This was his beautiful Ausi, who shared his life with him and would to the end. They had made her into a thrall again, but there wouldn't be a third time. Behind him stood the mass of thralls, panting, expectant.

Indistinct sounds came in the window near Ausi and the other thrall women. They changed to wild shrieks and crashing when the thralls burst into the Christian building and smashed it. Ausi suddenly felt in her heart that Holme was nearby. So the new Christ had finally heard her voice and had told Holme. Ausi laughed out loud with happiness and gratitude. The other women looked at her in terror and tried to quiet her down.

The uproar died away again, and the fear that Holme would leave without saving her seized her. She didn't consider for a moment that he might get killed. He was Holme, whom no one could vanquish, and now Christ was with him too, the real Christ. That was why she hadn't gotten any help when Geire raped her; Christ was with Holme and He couldn't be in two places at once, even though they said He could. Geire would answer for his actions when the time came.

The silence scared her; she listened but could hear only a weak murmuring and then a woman's scream. Ausi yelled as loud as she could twice. The other women thralls jumped on her and dragged her from the window, covering her mouth. In their stupidity, they believed that only inside the building were they safe from the dangerous man who now lay in wait outside.

At the first resounding blow, she knew that Holme had come. It echoed exquisitely in her ears because she knew it was Holme. Christ was gentle, but when He wanted something like this put to rights, He had to use Holme.

Another door was smashed apart before the one trapping her caved in under a single blow. There was soon a huge hole in it, and an ax chopped wildly at the edges. The thrall women cowered in a corner, frightened to death, even though Ausi kept explaining to them that the man who had come wasn't dangerous for thralls. She stood in the middle of the floor, and when the last piece of the door fell, she rushed out and threw her arms around Holme, who looked at her, astounded and out of breath. The thralls around them laughed good-naturedly but were still jealous. Most of them didn't have a family.

Ausi's eyes searched apprehensively until she saw Tora standing among the thralls. She met her daughter's eyes, no longer hateful but not yet gentle either. It was difficult for Tora to forget the baptism that she had been subjected to, but now she might have her revenge. Holme stood with sledgehammer in hand; that surely meant that the enemies had been struck to the ground and all would be well. Holme and Tora hadn't spoken a word to her, but she felt they wanted her back. Otherwise, why had they come and rescued her?

During all the chaos, Holme hadn't once forgotten his responsibility for the crazed band following him wherever he went. There were many men, but few women. Numerous women thralls were crouching here, pressing themselves against the wall while they looked at him in terror. Most of them were young or middle-aged. It would be good if they followed along to the mainland. They'd be needed there.

He quickly explained to Ausi what he was thinking, and she was willing to talk with the women at once. Many of them didn't understand, but some of them came over reluctantly, once they heard about the impending freedom at their own farmstead. No one would violate them; they'd get their pick of the men who didn't have women.

Loaded down with valuables and provisions, and most of them chewing some kind of food, the band of thralls returned to the open area. The surviving priest stood alone outside his devastated church. He said in a loud, trembling voice that they would get their just reward for what they had perpetrated against Christ and His servants. Their days were numbered. A gust of wind passed over the shrine, engulfing him with sacrificial smoke. The heathens were pleased with that response from the ancient gods, who were not afraid of Christ. Many axes and spears were raised against the priest, but Holme said a few words and the band, still eating, filed past the priest on both sides; he didn't budge from the spot.

Ausi turned around and watched the priest walk into his church through the broken door. He didn't fear for himself, but he still knew nothing about the real Christ—the one who felt like fire in your chest and made you run instead of walk.

No guard stood at the gate, and the thralls streamed out and down to the boats. The women and the feeblest men got to row across first. The chieftain might be in town gathering everyone together to stop the crossing. But two women, mother and daughter, refused to go without the dark, silent leader, whom they watched with love and admiration in their eyes.

But there wasn't a sound from town; it stood there in the quiet, late morning sun, and no trace of what had happened in the morning hours could be seen from the shore. A few figures were standing in the town gate, watching the thralls' departure. A group of warriors was standing on the rocks by the fortress, but they often stood there, looking in every direction. Maybe they were watching the thralls, happy they were leaving now that their work was done.

The first thing Geire noticed when he came to was a pair of bare, gray feet. He gradually remembered what had happened and figured out that he was lying between the feet of the thralls. They probably thought he was dead. If they knew he was still alive, they'd surely beat him to death like a dog with their clubs. His foggy brain tried to follow what was happening, but suddenly, all the gray feet around him took to flight, all rushing in the same direction, stomping and making an uproar, violently trampling him. Thralls! He had challenged them with an ax in his hand to exact revenge on their leader and scare the others away, but that's not how things had turned out.

Geire was used to punishing thralls and dogs with a stick. You didn't use a sword or a spear against them. But that smith had put a will in them along with the dangerous idea that they were just as good as their masters. That could do a lot of harm and cause a lot of unrest.

Geire saw the feet disappear behind the building after they had knocked the wind out of him by trampling heavily on his stomach and chest. Why didn't anyone drive the thralls from the chieftain's yard? Where would it all end if everyone yielded before them? It was like a bad dream, an impossibility—the thralls had taken up weapons and could harry wherever they wanted. If their leader at least were cut down, it would be easy enough to scare them into submission.

He tried struggling to his feet, but was still too exhausted. He could see the thralls returning, and walking beside the smith was his wife, the thrall Geire had raped that very morning. She still aroused that desire in him as he lay there half-dead. But Ausi didn't see Geire and that probably saved his life. He wanted to stay alive so that someday he could get the upper hand in battle with the thralls and especially the dangerous smith.

When he finally got to his feet, his face covered with dried blood, the door to the chieftain's house was opened for him, but Geire walked by in disdain. He wanted to show them that he wasn't afraid of the thralls no matter what. He limped past those standing in the town gate and approached the shore. The last boats had just set out, but he yelled a threat across the water and then saw the smith rest on his oars. His wife talked animatedly to him and soon he rowed on without answering.

Before long half the town was on shore, talking about what had happened and what ought to be done. Thralls had never dared act this way before. What were things coming to? It wouldn't be pleasant for anyone running into them on the mainland after they arrived, flushed with victory.

Most of the smiths and craftsmen stayed in town rather than follow Holme and the thralls toward an uncertain fate on the mainland. They weren't afraid of the consequences; they weren't defenseless, and the town needed them, both for its own sake and for the sake of business. They would gladly have seen Holme stay and take over the largest smithy, but that could no longer happen after the morning's events. Maybe another time, when there was a new chieftain in the town.

A couple of the new women thralls were wary of the whistling, unfamiliar forest that they'd be hidden in, perhaps forever. They were allowed to turn back; no one tried to stop them, though numerous jealous and disappointed eyes watched them go. Even Ausi felt for a moment the old fear of disappearing into the woods for good. To that point, she had kept reminding herself about the new Christ who'd be there to help them with everything, He who understood Holme and worked along with him, although Holme still didn't realize it. He'd be there in the forests, and for her sake, He'd probably help the thralls, whom every man now had a right to kill. Holme had been in the same position ever since robbing the Christian storehouse and distributing the grain, but there was a difference—no man would dare try killing him.

Ausi could sense the hesitancy of the two women once they had almost reached the shore. Some of the men sensed it too and encouraged them to come back. But they couldn't make up their minds and sat down where they were while the group continued down the forest road. No boats were coming after them from town yet. Probably nothing would be done before the king's order had been received.

That evening, they passed one of the farmsteads where a farmer had joined them to fight the Christians. The people there were standing outside silently and anxiously, aware that their master hadn't returned. A question to the dark figure at the front went unanswered. The thralls were emaciated and almost naked, but they looked happy as they talked or sang. They might have killed the free farmers who had joined them and then stolen their weapons, provisions, and possessions.

At sunset they stopped for the night. Holme had been looking for a good place for a long time, and he finally saw a sparkling vein of water running out from under a low-hanging rock and disappearing in a meadow of green, tender grass. He had passed by here once in the middle of the summer, and the meadow had been full of white, woolly balls on every stem. The water was fresh and cold there. The thralls stood in rows with their pails while Tora slurped from her hand on the rock above them.

Farther up, it was dry under the branches, and they lay down on the twigs in rows with their few tattered clothes on top of them. They were all happy and talked about the future when they'd walk as free men on their own land. They would rather fight and die in battle against their old masters than return to thralldom. They had weapons, and Holme knew how to do everything.

Ausi found a place for herself and her family away from the thralls' camp. All day she had been thinking about evening and night when she would tell Holme what had happened to her that morning. He would understand that she had done everything she could to get away, and when she lay pinned to the floor, unable to defend herself further, she had repressed those feelings that had built up so long inside her and had wanted to come out with the rapist's movements. She had been able to, too, but she still felt uneasy all day. Holme would have all the warmth she could give him now.

The thrall women went off by themselves to sleep, and she suggested quietly to Holme that the men should leave them alone. They'd choose among the men for themselves soon; she had already noticed some of them looking at each other warmly. If someone else stepped in there would be discontent and fighting among the men. Holme thought it good advice, and none of the thralls objected when he said they should let the women sleep by themselves. Holme didn't order them to do anything, but instead he talked with them as equals, and so they wanted to do as he asked. But they turned their heads often to the women's camp, and many of them lay awake hoping to see one of the women go off somewhere so a man would follow her.

When a younger woman finally got up, several heads popped up among the men, but she took only a couple of steps, and then came a hissing noise when she squatted in the moss. They envied Holme and strained to hear, but he was too far away. The only sound was from a gentle breeze passing through the great forest.

Once Tora had fallen asleep and the time had come, Ausi felt she should keep quiet about what had happened to her that morning. It seemed meaningless at that point; she hadn't let go at all. Holme was so calm and his eyes so gentle. She didn't want to see them turn stern and threatening again.

He didn't ask anything about her life while they had been apart and didn't say much about his own. Ausi had managed to place a clump of trees between them and the thralls, but still she listened in that direction before pulling Holme to her. Her body quivered, and she smiled more tenderly at him than ever before. They both turned their heads, listened to Tora's breathing and peered at her face through the darkness. Then all that could be heard was the rivulet gently rippling on the rocks and the soft rustling of leaves under Ausi's body.

After Holme gently freed himself from the arms of the sleeping Ausi, he lay for a long time listening to the sounds of the night in the woods—the murmur of the spring, which always sounded the same, the forest's almost imperceptible sigh, the whispering which never quite died away but inhered in the silence itself, and now another ordinary sound from the thralls. He tried to plan what he would do for them so they might all have a roof over their heads and something to live on. The first winter would be the hardest to survive. Holme didn't have many pigs—they wouldn't last long. He had an uneasy feeling that they might have to resort to robbing and plundering. And that would bring more pursuers, more dangers. Only merchants and farmers could plunder and steal without consequences. It meant death for thralls to commit the same crimes freemen did.

They could probably get meat in the woods but not bread. Everyone would look to him when they lacked anything. He was like a father to them. He had wanted to live alone with his family where they had once been thralls, but it wasn't going to work out that way. The thralls would offer sacrifices to the wooden gods and Ausi would call on Christ, but when danger was at hand, they would all come to him. And he would have to help as best he could; he couldn't say no to a thrall when he remembered his own thralldom.

Once during the night he heard a powerful snorting in the forest and then a lumbering run. It might be a bear, but it probably wouldn't attack so many. It could be a moose, too, that was just about to walk out there and suddenly caught the scent. Wild boars were the most dangerous of all; they attacked blindly and viciously, whether there was one or a whole herd. During the winter all those animals would be needed as game. Many hungry men would eat their flesh.

Geire's hatred was smoldering inside as he watched the thralls disappear toward the mainland. He no longer wanted to sail with the ship, preparing instead to stay until he had gotten even with the smith. The Vikings would have to find another warrior to take his place. He would never forget that the thralls had beaten him to the ground with their clubs and trampled on him with their bare feet.

Later, he sat with his sister and her son in Holme's house, and they talked about what had happened. They criticized both the chieftain, who couldn't control a pack of thralls, and the warriors, who had refused to obey him. At the same time, Geire couldn't help feeling a certain admiration for the thralls' courage. He had always considered them whimpering, crawling dogs, but these hadn't retreated for anything. However, it was Holme who held them together; without him they'd be the same helpless herd as before.

They also considered the possibility of Holme's returning alone during the night. They had recently seen his sledgehammer open doors, so they couldn't sleep easily in his house anymore. Geire wasn't afraid for himself, but the smith wouldn't spare the woman or the boy if Geire fell under the sledgehammer's blows. Then there'd be no one left to avenge them.

He had seen Svein's terror of the smith and that disturbed him. It had to have come from the mother's endless stories and warnings when he was a child. He'd be full-grown soon and strong for his age. He could handle a weapon, too, and one of them had to kill the smith.

His sister, the thralls' former owner, wallowed in her own terrible, bitter thoughts. She had been so sure she was going to see Holme, her hated enemy, hacked down and his wife delivered into her hands again, this time along with their daughter. But they had been able to row away, right in front of her eyes, and there wasn't a judge at the assembly who could do a thing about it. What had things come to when thralls could do exactly as they pleased? She also felt like she was homeless even though she owned her enemy's house. As long as he was alive and free, they wouldn't have one single peaceful night's sleep, afraid every minute of a thunderous blow against the door.

Everything had turned sour on her after her first husband died and was buried at the settlement. She hadn't made sacrifices to any god since then; maybe that was the reason for all this. The scorched god on the slope at the settlement might be taking revenge on her. That had to be it; she should have realized it before. She should at least have made an offering to him when she passed by the settlement after escaping thralldom in the foreign land. But instead she had despised him for his helplessness.

Now, though, she couldn't get back there to set things right. Besides, there was so little to sacrifice in these times of adversity. Half of Holme's silver had already been used up, and it was going to be a rough winter. The blackened god would keep standing on the stone, conjuring new problems for her. There was no god in Holme's house, and if there had been, she wouldn't have dared turn to him.

With an aching heart that afternoon when Geire and Svein were out, she took a fist full of silver, tied it in a piece of cloth, and walked to the shrine opposite the Christian church. Maybe the huge god there was the most powerful of gods and could keep the one at the settlement from visiting misfortunes on her. She would talk with his servant in the temple about it.

The Christian church was quiet and deserted. The bell tower that Holme had chopped to the ground was still lying there, but the bells were gone. Curiosity prompted her to walk up to the door and look in after glancing furtively at the wooden god. Everything was smashed to bits inside and the valuables had disappeared. A strange sound echoed in the empty hall, and presently she saw the Christian priest on his knees among the debris. His face was turned upward—he was probably calling down his god's punishment on Holme and the thralls. She hoped his god would have the power to destroy them.

The priest seemed to sense someone in the doorway and got up to look. She started to pull back, but he was beside her in an instant, showing her the destruction with a sorrowful smile. He didn't know this heathen woman with the hard face, but he showed her the disaster that had befallen him anyway. His fellow priest lay dead in the chieftain's courtyard, and he was no doubt feeling threatened and forsaken in this pagan country.

The woman expected him to blame his god for what it couldn't or chose not to stop, but instead he spoke even warmer and more appreciative words about him. She suddenly remembered something that had happened while her squat, powerful husband was still alive. A hailstorm had come and struck down his beautiful grain, even though veils of sacrificial smoke had floated around the fertility god. Moments later the chieftain, consumed with rage, chopped the god to bits, railing against him for his worthlessness as he did so. But after he had calmed down, he had gone looking for a suitable tree to carve a new god out of. He had looked so high up the trunks that his beard had stood straight out.

She didn't pay much attention to what the priest was saying, but she did listen to his soft voice with surprise and pleasure. She had never heard such gentleness in a man's voice, had not even known that it could exist. And after all he had lost! It wasn't easy to understand him.

She didn't see anyone moving in the shrine of the wooden god, and she needed to talk with someone who could advise and help her. When the foreign priest asked why she was at the ravaged church, she told him everything in her own abrupt way—about the blackened god standing on the stone far away at the settlement and sending evil into her life. About Holme and Ausi and all they had inflicted upon her. She was going to offer a sacrifice to the god in the other temple so that he might divert the misfortune from her and let it fall on her enemies instead.

When she had finished, the priest started in about the powerless wooden gods and the living Christ. But the woman could see His demolished church; no one could make her believe in His power when He couldn't even drive away a pack of thralls. How could he save her from the revenge of the settlement's god? The priest assured her that Christ would do that without asking anything in return, but that made her even more suspicious. Who would do something for nothing?

She listened silently to the priest's words, but they were like water on a duck's back. She was looking toward the temple the whole time, and finally one of the attendants came out of the shrine, yawned, looked up at the wooden god, and began cleaning him up after the morning sacrifice. The heathen woman was getting restless. She looked once more at the devastation of the Christian church, and then walked toward the untouched shrine of the wooden god. He was obviously the strongest one; he and his house were still standing there undamaged.

The priest watched her go, thinking again that the work was lost. It wasn't his work, but the one who had started it had said that it was standing firm on its foundation; it was just a matter of moving it along. But now Christ surely wasn't left in a single heathen heart, not with the church and all the sparkling things in it gone. No one had understood or wished to understand the inner meaning of the message. As far as he was concerned, the heathens could keep their wooden gods until the end of time. He'd go back home before he too was cut down. The one who had kindled the light in the north could return himself to keep it burning.

With the first ship, he would send a report of what had happened and request a replacement. Then his fellow priest, who now wore the crown of martyrdom, would be buried with as much dignity as possible among enemies and nominal Christians. The chieftain would still help, even if he hadn't been able to protect the church or the priest's life. The thralls had defied him, and the warriors had refused to follow his orders and strike them down. This strange people had kings and chieftains, but ignored their orders and did as they pleased. He had heard stories that the people had more than once seized a king or chieftain and sacrificed him when some great misfortune had come on the land;[12] he wondered if such a people would ever become Christian.

He felt like a tiny, flickering candle in an endless night. Could he get himself out of this? He didn't want to die here and lie wait-

12. E. O. G. Turville-Petre, *Myth and Religion of the North* (New York: Holt, Rinehart, & Winston, 1964), p. 253, points out that the king represented the relevant Norse god, even incorporated the god within him. He may therefore have been sacrificed in the autumn so that he could revive again in the spring.

ing for the Day of Judgment among heathen burial mounds. Maybe Christ wouldn't even bother with this place, and the everlasting silence would settle over it. An eternal oblivion was already whispering across the burial mounds outside the town; he had sensed that as a threat and as challenging the power of Christ. Maybe God never intended this land to see the light. And so He had let thralls destroy His church and turn His disciple into a martyr.

The heathen woman was coming out of the temple with a smug look on her face. She had probably been promised help by the servant of the wooden god. She folded up the piece of cloth she had brought the silver in, looked respectfully up at the lofty wooden god, and walked away without giving the Christian church a single glance.

The smith's wife, Ausi, had once told a story about a Christian priest who had labored there in town but had ultimately been sacrificed when he had tried to burn down the heathens' greatest temple on the mainland. The monk hadn't believed the story, but it was beginning to seem plausible. There certainly had been many men during the course of time who had believed they were called as apostles to the heathens, but had been lost forever in the forests and at the heathens' sacrificial altars.

He didn't want to become one of them; he would request a replacement as fast as possible. He yearned for Christ to return him to his homeland so he could convince everyone that his mission was hopeless.[13]

When Holme and the band of thralls started getting close to the cave, he took a detour so they wouldn't discover it. He had a

13. Gautbert was driven from Sweden in about 845 and was not replaced until 851 (*Anskar,* chapter 19, p. 61).

vague feeling that someday he might need it again as a hiding place for himself and his family. There were many dangerous enemies who would never give him any peace as long as he was still alive.

With great expectation and happiness, Ausi saw again the place where she had spent her childhood and lived in servitude. The whole band stopped at the edge of the forest to look down on the yellow grain swaying in Holme's fields. Ausi saw lush grass and shrubs with red berries now where the buildings had once stood. The millstone that she had ground grain with so often was still standing in the same place, and a shower had left a little water in the indentation.

The thralls wandered happily around the slope and looked expertly at the grain where it was still unaffected by the blight. They picked up handfuls of earth and let it run between their fingers, grunting appreciatively. While there were a lot of things unusable here, a good number of people could still have bread. A couple of men were already trying their luck with Holme's fishing gear at the shore. Others stood looking at the mounds in the burial grove while they exchanged opinions about them. Muddy, black paths had been worn by the hooves of the pigs under the alder bushes by the shore.

Farther up the hillside, the blackened wooden god was standing on his rock, and someone had already placed a couple of tiny morsels from the last meal in front of him. Birds flew back and forth between the trees and the god, carrying the small bits of food in their beaks.

The thralls were prancing around like carefree children, but Holme looked at them with concern. There were just too many of them for one spot. He had seen a building at the other farmstead that was about ready to cave in, and wild grain was flourishing in the old fields; some of them would have to go there. They could fish and hunt, and when the grain was harvested, it would be divided up equally among all of them. He'd go along himself and help them get started.

The women had stopped on the slope, talking or lying on their backs with their eyes closed. A few of them would go with the men to the other farmstead. A new building would soon be built for them, and the men could live in the old one for a while.

When the time had come, Holme walked down to the shore and looked for an equal number of white and gray stones to put in a wooden bowl. He called the men together and said that those who picked gray stones would move on, those with white stones would stay. The same would be true for the women. Ausi's suggestion that she be allowed to keep one of the younger girls she had grown fond of was turned down.

But when their turn came, the women indicated that several of them had already made their choice. They walked self-consciously over to stand near the men they had secretly had an eye on. They were full of anxiety about not being able to go where their men went. Some even went without bothering with the drawing of lots, thinking that life would probably be about the same in both places. Only the youngest, almost a child like Tora, looked anxiously at the bearded men and stood next to Ausi for protection. No one ordered her to come along to the other farmstead, and Ausi gladly took her to her house.

Early the next morning, Holme walked on with the men, women, and tools. He walked alone at the head of the group, followed by the women and then the men, who were laughing and singing and ringing the little Christian bell. From the settlement Ausi could hear the ringing grow weaker and finally die away in the forest. Holme would probably be back again the next day.

Tora and the young girl were asleep in the house, the men were out in the woods cutting down trees for the new building, and the women were wandering here and there. Ausi went off by herself, looking at everything and recalling things that had happened in different places.

She hadn't felt this happy and safe for a long time. The old uneasiness that the stranger had infused in her was gone, now that she knew he was Christ Himself. There was nothing more she had to know; no matter how bad things might look, he would eventually fix them all. That's why she was there with her loved ones. The Christ she knew would never stand between her and Holme.

She stopped by the pile of ashes that had once been the two thrall huts. She had given birth in one of them to Tora, whom Stor and Tan had carried off into the forest. She had still been afraid of Holme back then and bitter, too, because he had done nothing to stop them. Instead, he did what no man had ever done before for his woman and baby. Stor and Tan were dead now; Holme had told her during the night that they had tried to ax him in his sleep, even though he had meant them no harm. They shared a grave here at the settlement where they had lived all their lives. But that was all right; they wouldn't dare come back to do any mischief as long as Holme was around.

She also stopped by the wooden god, and a little gray bird flew off with a crumb of bread in its beak. She wouldn't offer him anything, although the settlement was hers now. He could do nothing against Christ and Holme. Anyway, she would ask Holme to lift him down from the rock and take him away. Otherwise, the people living here now might give him food they could make better use of themselves. She looked for a moment at the blackened clump of wood that still had the human shape, and she remembered when the chieftain had called in a skillful craftsman to carve and paint him. That was just before Tora was born.

There was no sign of the pigs yet, but they would probably come back at night. The flies buzzing around the tracks in the warm mud indicated they had been home the last few nights. Holme had let them out before going to town to rescue her. The pigs would come home in the evening; she knew their habits well and knew they'd stop at the edge of the forest, blinking mistrustfully at the new life in the settlement. They probably couldn't be called in before Holme, whom they knew, came back.

The three largest burial mounds all looked alike now since thick grass had grown on even the newest of them. She thought about the stocky chieftain lying in his; he had condemned her baby to be abandoned in the woods. He had hated Holme and hadn't wanted to let the baby live because it was Holme's, even though thrall children had been needed at the settlement. Now he lay there in a mound and Holme was in charge. It was amusing when what happened was the opposite of what the powerful wanted. He certainly wouldn't be able to rise up and do them any harm; she had seen the fire consume all but his largest bones.

It was quiet and beautiful down among the mounds, and the wild strawberries growing on the sides of the mounds were blooming for the second time. Adjacent to the mounds were several smaller graves of women, and farther away there were numerous tiny, uneven mounds. There lay all the thralls who had died or been killed at the settlement. The chieftain in the mound had many warriors so he could attack and plunder passing ships. The mightiest of them, Stenulf, had been killed by Holme with an ax and now lay under a high mound of round stones near the cave.

Ausi had seen all that was left from her days as a thrall. The landing was falling apart and the logs turning white. The little boat the thrall had stolen still lay there, its bottom filled with warm rainwater. Big round rocks that used to be underwater were now up on land, whitening in the sun. Ausi climbed on them and they almost burned her bare feet. A spry, ice-gray bird with a long, fluttering tail landed on a log and looked at her with cocked head before resuming its airy hunt among the warm logs and stones.

There was one more place Ausi wanted to see again. She looked around self-consciously and walked along the shore a while. Between a few alder bushes was a small chamberlike area where the grass was green far into the autumn. She stopped, looked at the place, and smiled. Holme had dragged her in there one autumn. Then winter came, and in the summer, Tora was born. She had fought him off as long as she could, but two of her friends had seen them through an opening in the bushes, and they said she had finally thrown her arms around his neck. She didn't remember that but didn't think it impossible.

There she stood now, glad it was Holme and no one else who had taken her. She leaned over and caressed the grass before returning to the settlement. It was damp and she remembered that her skirt had clung to her back that time after she had broken loose and stood up.

After a mild winter when the lake didn't freeze over a summer came with a good harvest. The people at the farmsteads didn't see strangers too often and they heard nothing from the outside. Then one day a man came by Holme's place and said that the blight had attacked the grain again, for the third straight year, and that many people had starved to death during the winter and spring. There had also been much less seed to be sown, so the harvest would have an even smaller yield than during the last two years of famine.

The man looked in surprise at the dazzling grain swaying in Holme's fields. He recognized Holme and knew what had happened in town, but he kept it to himself; instead, he praised all he saw as he ate their food. But he took careful note of everything so he could tell about it when he got back. He could see how it all fit together now and looked with terror-stricken eyes at the blackened god that Holme hadn't bothered to take off the rock. It was clear to him that the blight had swept across the land directly from that grimy god and that Holme was responsible. Everyone believed that Holme knew more than other people did. This was a great discovery, and once the man had eaten his fill, he turned back toward town instead of continuing his journey.

Holme watched him and for an instant felt a dark sense of foreboding. But he couldn't do anything against a man seeking hospitality. A whole year had passed since they had settled down here, and he had begun to hope that all would be forgotten. The chieftain surely wouldn't want to waste time and warriors hunting thralls in the woods. He might even be expecting them to come to town sooner or later to barter for things they couldn't get any place else. Many of the thralls at both farmsteads were running short of clothes and shoes. A couple of the least-recognized men might be able to travel to town and trade for cloth and skins without risking anything happening to them. But Holme couldn't go to town. Everyone knew him.

The chieftain listened pensively to the man's animated story. The chieftain still believed in Christ, even though the last priest had lost heart and gone home. Replacements would come as soon as they felt called to this difficult mission—at least that's what a message said from the monk directing everything from his cloister in the far-off land.[14] He asked the chieftain and the few others still clinging to Christ to keep faith. The reward would be great and glorious in its time, and they would triumph over their adversaries.

But even though Christ might be the most powerful, the chieftain didn't take lightly the wooden gods' abilities to be revenged. He had seen all-too-much proof of what they could do. He could well imagine the evil smith using the charred god on the stone to send disease on the grain throughout the land. It had to be true: blight from a black god, a black god for a dark man like Holme. That man had to be destroyed, along with his god, if starvation was to be stopped from ultimately laying waste to the entire land. The blight had spread more and more each year.

That same day, the chieftain himself was rowed to the king's farmstead to make the situation clear to him. The king was walking around his grain fields, looking with dismay at the pitiful stalks where the blight had taken hold. He had ordered the fertility god moved out into the middle of the fields, where it stood, gazing across the lake with the stalks brushing against its base. It had been there since the grain had sprouted, but it either couldn't or wouldn't stop the blight.

The king listened to his chieftain's story and soon became convinced that they had finally discovered where the blight came from. He too remembered the smith, having once been provoked by his indifference and defiance. The smith was also an outlaw from many years before; even so, the king still suggested that the chieftain take him alive and bring him before the assembly. He

14. I.e., Ansgar.

might have things to say that would be useful to know. The king ordered that Holme and everyone with him be brought to town—and as fast as possible, if any of the harvest was to be saved. He also mentioned a reward for the man who had made this important discovery.

As had happened many years before when the short-legged chieftain fell in battle, a man came running through the forest, panting, a terrible message in his mouth. Coughing and wheezing, he rushed to Holme and told his story. He had been in an outlying field at the other farmstead and had seen it suddenly surrounded by warriors, all on horseback, and he recognized some of them. They were the king's guard, and the chieftain himself was riding at their head. The thrall had seen his gray beard under the golden helmet. He said that no one else had gotten out alive.

Holme listened with apprehension and anger and realized there'd be no more peace. It would be pointless to try to fight the warrior troop with axes and spears. They had probably gone to the other farmstead first by mistake, or perhaps they had been confident that no one would escape to spread the news.

Holme rang the bell to call the people together for a brief meeting. The enemies were many and strong; everyone agreed that there was no point in fighting them in the open. But some of the people looked sad and some enraged because of the year they had spent at the settlement living a good and peaceful life, and because of the whispering, golden grain that would soon be ripe.

Soon the last of them disappeared into the forest, loaded down with their possessions, and the settlement was empty. The door of the pig sty stood open. The pigs had been driven into the forest, and the fire pit was still hissing softly from the water it had been doused with. Holme turned around and looked back at the settlement as he had so often done before. He couldn't remember any more how many times he had run away from it and then returned. But he didn't feel at home anywhere else.

Holme returned alone after taking his people a good distance into the woods. Ausi calmly watched him arrive; she had been convinced that Christ, in the shape of the stranger, would be walking beside him and protecting him. But the men were dour and irritable; one of them suddenly growled that they should have stayed and fought. The forest was whispering and the birds were singing around the band of thralls sitting there on the ground, but a powerful enemy was threatening the freedom in the forest they had fought for and enjoyed for a year.

Holme had to wait in his hiding place for a while before he heard them coming. A horse whinnied, probably catching the settlement's scent. Then Holme heard more than saw the riders fan out and surround the settlement so no one could escape.

He could hear horses snorting and twigs cracking in several places at once, and then the horses flashed into sight and disappeared. At a loud yell, they all thundered toward the settlement, many of them riding straight through the fields of golden grain. Holme laughed sardonically as he watched them whirling around among the empty buildings, searching for victims. The troop of warriors they had sent against him and his thralls was large, but as always, the forest sheltered the fugitive and the outlaw.

Holme stayed put until the warriors got off their horses and gathered around the chieftain to confer with him. It was moving toward evening; they would probably spend the night there. But he had to get back to his people. He had already planned to double back to the farmstead the riders had just left and see how much damage they had done. Surely they'd take another route home.

Just then, he heard men coming from the same direction, so he took cover again. Five or six horsemen rode up with thralls tied behind their horses, both men and women. He was close enough to hear their labored breathing and see their bulging eyes. One of the women was carrying her baby and was trying to nurse it as she ran. The thralls' legs were bleeding from cuts and scratches they had gotten on branches and stones in the forest.

Holme ground his teeth and then ran through the forest as he had run only once before in his life. He still didn't know exactly what he was going to do, but he knew he'd act that night. They were dragging his people behind their horses, people whose only crime was choosing to fend for themselves and live in peace.

Ausi heard him coming before she could see him, and she too remembered the night he had raced three times between the cave and the settlement. The thralls were waiting in a place not very far from the cave, but no one but she and Holme knew about it. When she caught sight of him, she could see he was running as fast as the last time, though he was much older now. He glided like a shadow across the ground. Most of the others had settled down to rest while they waited for him, and some were already asleep.

The other men, having been free only for the past year, were just glad their companions were still alive. They felt no outrage at having been dragged behind horses; their own thralldom was still too fresh in their minds. But Ausi was aware that it had been a long time since she had seen Holme's face so hard and bitter. Even so, he could expect nothing but death for the people from the other farmstead.

The man who had brought Holme the news was allowed to lead the women and children to the other farmstead; the men went with Holme. He had no idea what they were going to do; attacking the horsemen would be insane. But the coming night would be the thralls' and outlaws' ally, made for quiet steps, silent shadows, and the flight of spears.

There was still a little daylight left when they reached the edge of the forest. Holme scouted ahead while the men waited just inside the forest. The warriors had surely posted a guard.

When he got close enough to the settlement, Holme could see that something was going on. Horses were neighing, a couple of warriors were coming up the path from the lake, talking, and a couple of others were standing by the fields of grain. Something was missing, and it took a moment for Holme to figure out what it was. The wooden god on the rock was gone. The warriors had probably knocked him down, angry because their prey had flown.

He could discern a larger group of horses and people near the grove by the house. It was the thralls and their women—still bound to the horses—sitting on the ground. They kept turning toward the forest, as if looking for help. In all likelihood, they knew Holme and the others were still free. Occasionally, he could hear a baby cry. Two or three warriors stood in front of the horses.

In the woods behind him, Holme heard sounds—a stifled cough, a breaking twig, a whisper. Dark figures scampered from tree to tree, and soon he was surrounded. The thralls just couldn't wait, and he smiled in the darkness at their zeal. The warriors had posted no guard, either by the forest or by the lake, probably because they felt nothing but disdain for the thralls who had escaped their grasp.

Moments later, Holme and the thralls heard the chieftain come out and give the warriors their orders. He said they'd sleep until daybreak and then begin tracking Holme and the thralls. They couldn't afford to return to town without the smith, the most dangerous man in the land. Holme heard the familiar voice say something about Christ being with them on their journey so it had to succeed. Besides, this mission was to save the whole land from famine. He finished by asking for Christ's protection during the night.

The statement about famine surprised Holme. How could capturing and killing him and the thralls save the land from the blight? As usual, the Christians were going to involve Christ in everything and then blame the heathens or the wooden gods if anything went wrong.

The warriors disappeared into the buildings, and soon the chewing and snorting of the horses were the only sounds that could be heard. The guard standing in front of the horses would move now and then, stopping and looking out over the lake or turning toward the forest and listening. The captured thralls had lain down, and every once in a while you could hear the sound of women sobbing. The sweet smell of ripened grain grew stronger in the humid night air, reaching the men hiding behind the trees.

The guard never went behind the horses to check on the prisoners. Perhaps he didn't like the silent weeping of the women, or perhaps the darkness of the night and the silence made him fearful that one of the men might break free and sneak up on him with a knife. Once he took out some food, smacking his lips as he ate. The thralls who hadn't had anything to eat or drink since morning could hear him, and their own hunger pangs increased.

Once he reached the grove it wasn't too far for Holme to crawl. A horse turned its head and looked indifferently at him through the darkness as he emerged from the foliage and crawled stealthily through the grass. His biggest concern was that the thralls in their surprise would give him away. Even so, he might still be able to get them loose and into the woods before the warriors could get to their feet and attack.

The first thrall to catch sight of him gasped, and for a moment Holme stopped in his tracks. A whisper moved quickly among the people lying on the ground; the women stopped crying, and heads slowly bent forward straining to see. A knife appeared passing from hand to hand, and as it moved the straps fell away from raw, swollen wrists.

Once they were free, the prisoners had a single thought—the woods. Some leaped up and fled on wobbly legs; others, unable to stay on their feet, fell and crawled toward the forest. The mother's hurried movements woke the baby and it started screaming. The horses grew restless, and suddenly the guard gave a loud yell and, before Holme could stop him, ran toward the buildings. The four horses that had been cut loose sensed it and started galloping across the slope.

Holme was the last to leave. He watched as the warriors came tumbling out of the buildings, fumbling with their clothes and weapons. The horses that were still tied had spooked—several of them yanked loose and galloped wildly around. The thralls had enough time to get to the edge of the forest, and those who couldn't run fast enough were held up or dragged along by the others. The baby kept screaming, and that meant they had to get out of hearing range fast.

A chase couldn't easily begin before dawn, so, after he made certain that everyone would meet at the other farmstead, Holme turned back again. He wanted to find out what the warriors were up to so he'd know how to respond. If they decided to ride to the other farmstead again, he'd somehow have to get there before them.

Once he was alone, walking back through the forest, Holme felt a great sense of relief and happiness at having been able to set the thralls free. The danger wasn't over yet, but they had bought valuable time. Maybe the enemy would finally tire of the hunt and let them live as they pleased in the forest. They would never bother anybody but, instead, would help all the outlawed, wretched people who happened along the roads.

Soon Holme was back at the edge of the forest and could see the commotion in the darkness among the buildings. Some of the horses had not been caught yet and were running scared, crazed with fear, rearing up when the men got near them and pawing violently at the air. Voices were raised excitedly, and Holme could hear the guard defending himself as best he could. He told them that the blackened wooden god they had toppled from the stone had come sneaking up in the darkness to free the prisoners. Then it had charged him—he had only narrowly escaped.

Holme heard his own name mentioned when the chieftain said that the black god hadn't budged. The one who had freed the prisoners was Holme, whom most of them knew from town. In the darkness, he might look like the black wooden god. But Christ was stronger than all the other gods, and when daylight came He would help them. Until then, they must stay alert. No one knew what the smith would do next. He was undoubtedly in league with the evil powers living there in the forest, and the chieftain blamed himself for not putting a stronger guard over the thralls.

A moment later, about half the warriors went back into the buildings, while the other half stayed outside, talking quietly and looking around. A soft light was shining above the fields, and fireflies danced in silent swarms. An occasional chirping from the young seabirds drifted up from the reeds below.

Countless thoughts passed through Holme's mind as he sat there at the forest's edge. They came out of the long ago, and he wasn't sure sometimes what had really happened. Many dreams and old plans had become mixed with his memories. He had been greatly mistreated and hunted, but he had fought back too. Many men had never gotten up again, but he had acted wrongfully only once. That was when the man had moved into the house outside town where Ausi and he had lived before. He had had a perfect right to move into the empty house, as much right as they had had. But Holme's ax had spoken before his mind could.

More than anything else, Holme would have chosen to live in the forest all his life and have a little farmstead with a smithy. But he hadn't been able to do that; instead he had been forced into violence. If everyone were free, there would be no need to fight and kill each other. No one had any idea how big the country was; there was enough for everybody. But no one was going to free a thrall, so they had had to fight for freedom as he had done. Then the chase was on, and it had been a freedom without peace.

But most of those who had been free for a while would rather fight and die than return to thralldom. And if anyone did return, he would never be the same; he would carry his freedom in his heart and search for the chance to reach it again. Their lords would never be able to sleep peacefully with thralls around who'd had a taste of freedom. When enough thralls had tasted, they would shove away everything that stood in the path of freedom.

If this thrall hunt failed, they might be left in peace for a while. But they'd always have to live with one eye on the forest and the other on the lake. If the freemen could understand, then the thralls could approach them calmly and suggest a truce. If the freemen would let the thralls live in the forest and come to town to barter occasionally, they would in turn never cause anybody any trouble. That way, all thralls would finally be free, and no difference would separate freemen and thralls. They were basically the same from the beginning anyway. A thrall was just as strong, sometimes stronger, than a freeman. One didn't dare do more than the other, and you couldn't tell the difference between a lord and a thrall once they took their clothes off.

Before dawn, Holme understood that freemen could never be reasoned with. There was only one way—to unite all the thralls in the land and kill every freeman who opposed the thralls' freedom. Many thralls, perhaps himself included, would fall in that struggle, but others could live on freely and happily on their farmsteads and in small forest clearings.

When the warriors gathered together again, Holme could hear the chieftain telling them that if they could just get Holme, the others didn't matter. With him out of the way, they'd make short work of the thralls. He also told them he would send men back to these farmsteads to harvest the crop for the king. As they could see, it was plentiful and untouched by the blight. But they wouldn't send anybody for the bell the thralls had hung up on the gable of the building to call each other with. They'd take it with them immediately.

The warriors ate their breakfast standing by their horses and drank water from the wooden tankards hanging on the saddles. They were in a good mood, kidding and cackling in their beards over the various ideas they kept coming up with for capturing Holme and the thralls. But the chieftain warned them to be careful; there wasn't a man among them who could take Holme alone, and the thralls would fight like wolves for their freedom. Those who had escaped from this farmstead were surely armed, and they knew what was waiting for them in town.

The chieftain turned down a warrior's suggestion that they destroy the charred wooden god. The clump of wood could do no harm by itself; Holme was calling forth the blight through it. If they could capture him, everything would go back to normal.

When they left, a man was sent ahead of them on foot to track the thralls through the moss and brush. After a while Holme recognized him and knew at once who was behind everything that was happening—the man who had come through the forest, eaten his food, and taken stock of everything on the farmsteads—he who afterward had gone back the same way he had come.

Holme watched him as closely as he could through the branches. He had a new goal now to add to all the others. He had to get even with that man when the time was right.

After the riders had disappeared into the forest, Holme crouched and ran down to the shore, took the small boat from the landing, and began rowing. Just outside the reeds, he put his back into it and the boat sped silently forward. It was closer by water than by land; even if the warriors rode straight to the other farmstead, he'd get there at the same time or ahead of them. But it should take them a while to find the thralls' tracks.

He soon rowed past the place where he and Ausi had stopped to rest during their escape from thralldom, and again everything seemed like a recurrent dream. But he couldn't help it; everything he did seemed inevitable—whether it meant striking a man down, or stepping to the side so he didn't trample an insect on the forest path.

But he didn't give any thought as to who was in control of all these things. The heathens said it was the wooden gods, the sun, or the stars; the Christians said it was their god. He didn't care about any of it; when the time came for him to do something, he always knew it.

The chieftain allowed the younger, more zealous warriors to ride in front through the forest, just behind the tracker, while he rode last. He was old and sure the thralls wouldn't attack; they would only defend themselves once they were caught.

He let his head hang so that his beard lay on his chest while the horse picked its own way through the rocks and thickets. He thought about the strange mission he had undertaken. Some inner sense had whispered to him the whole time that no mortal could send the blight, but he didn't mention it to the others. If the warriors believed otherwise, everything was easier. The thralls were guilty enough anyway. Never before had they tried fighting for freedom and then begun living like farmers. What would happen if they did that all through the country? But it was probably Holme's fault that they had done the things they had. Once he was gone, everything would fall back into the old familiar order.

The longer the chieftain thought about their nerve, the more he began to boil. Thralls living like lords! They should be whipped so they'd never pull a stunt like that again. It might be best to kill them all so they couldn't entice others to repeat what they had done. However, the king would decide in this matter.

If only Christ would help them with the capture. The day was clear and blue; He could see them all from heaven—the thralls fleeing and the warriors tracking through the forest. The priests said that He was omnipresent, so He could surely give them a hint about which way to ride. The tracker lost the track again and again, and the horsemen had to stand by until he sniffed it out. Sometimes he'd kneel down, groping in the grass and moss. A couple of times, he even put his nose down and sniffed like a dog. He should have used a dog instead; then tracking a pack of thralls would have been easy.

But Christ didn't help, maybe because so many of the warriors were still heathens. A few had been baptized before riding out on the thrall hunt, just in case, but not all of them. If the newly baptized fell, at least they could ascend to heaven, where Christ would help their souls. But the unbaptized would sleep forever. The wooden gods had no power to awaken their followers.

It was hard to understand how the thralls could escape in the dark of night with women and children. But their leader was friendly with the powers of darkness, and they probably helped him in the forest. That meant the chieftain and his men would have to catch the thralls while it was still day when Christ and all the gods of light held sway.

In a glade, the tracker triumphantly picked up some loose berries that indicated the thralls had passed there. But a lot of animals like bears and birds ate berries so they meant little. The chieftain had been convinced for a long time they were going the wrong way, and decided to take the lead himself—with Christ's help, of course.

He gathered his warriors around him in the next glade and told them his misgivings about the route they were taking. He pointed out too that Christ could see them and probably wanted to give them a sign. The warriors looked silently at him.

He bent his head back, making his beard stand out from his chin, looked up into the blue above the treetops, and prayed in a loud voice for Christ to show them the way. Afterward, he would show his gratitude with gifts to the church.

It was absolutely quiet for a moment, and the warriors sat motionless on their horses in anxious expectation. Then the clear, drawn-out cry of a bird emerged from deep in the forest to the right of the glade. A glow of triumph passed over the chieftain's face when he asked if everyone had heard it.

Most of the warriors' faces lit up with surprise or happiness, but a couple of the men were skeptical.

"It was just a bird," one of them said.

But the chieftain turned his horse toward the sound, and his voice expressed unshakable certainty when he said that Christ could respond in whatever tongue He wanted to. He was that powerful in comparison to the wooden idols. He was in all things and knew about everything before it happened.

It was already midday, and they hadn't gotten far following the crawling, hunched-over tracker. Now they moved quickly with the gray-haired chieftain riding proudly at the head of the troop. Christ had answered him and everything would be fine. He could approach the king with Holme and the thralls in tow, and then they'd get what was coming to them.

In the first daylight, the thralls saw again the farmstead they were sure they had left forever the day before when they had been dragged away behind horses. Nothing had been burned or stolen because the chieftain had planned to send people back here too to take charge of the fine grain, the most beautiful he had seen in many years. The grain had convinced him more than anything else that Holme and the thralls were in league with the powers of evil.

Ausi and Tora sat down with a view of the forest road to wait for Holme. Ausi prayed silently for Christ to accompany and protect him through the forest. She concentrated so hard that she conjured them in a vision. Holme was walking down the path with that gliding stride he always used in the forest. The stranger was walking among the bushes lining both sides of the path. He was only one man, but Ausi somehow saw him among the trees and stones on both sides of Holme.

She was certain everything would be fine. The chieftain was Christian, but not like the stranger and herself. He was like the last priests, those who had to make offerings and promises to get any help. Her Christ sat like a clear, joyous light in her chest. He wasn't austere and demanding like the last priests, but mild, and He understood everything, even whatever was called sin. She alone knew what He was like, but there was no one to tell. Not yet.

Most of the thralls lay down to rest after tending their wounds. A couple of the strongest men had walked down to the landing with fishing gear. A big, almost-new boat was tied at the landing, and the men were pleased to see no one had touched it while they had been away.

Tora lay down on the ground and was soon asleep. Ausi kept waiting for Holme to come out of the forest; Christ would be standing there at the edge, smiling as if to say, "Here you are." But even Ausi felt the weight and the fatigue after the night in the woods and all the tension. The edge of the forest grew dark and shimmered in a pleasant twilight.

Just as she was about to fall asleep, a shout came from the lake, and opening her eyes, she saw one of the men on the landing, pointing toward the east. Her first thought was that other enemies were approaching by water now that Holme wasn't home. But before she could get to her feet a boat glided out of the swath of fire in front of the sun, and she recognized instantly the figure bent over the oars. She had expected him to come through the forest! As always, Holme knew what was best—he and Christ.

Ausi quietly left the sleeping girl and ran down the slope to meet Holme. They could rest now, all three of them, after the hard night. Then they'd get up and get something to eat.

But even at a distance, she could tell there'd be no rest. Holme wasn't moving any faster than usual, but from his crouched position she could see that the danger wasn't over.

Holme had rowed about halfway when it occurred to him that his calculations were wrong. The warriors would track the people all the way to the farmstead. He had thought they'd give up and return to town, but he could see more clearly now. During the day, they'd have plenty of time to reach the farmstead even if they lost the track several times.

It angered him that his fatigue had kept him from seeing that. He was no old man and was responsible for a lot of people. Now there had to be either a fight or another escape into the woods with the riders on their heels. He'd let the men decide for themselves if they wanted to stay and fight. As for him, he was tired of fleeing like a wolf through the forest.

He was relieved to see the men on the landing when he approached. Everything seemed to be all right. The farmstead was close to a cove, and a short distance out was an islet with a grassy meadow and some trees. An idea struck him and he rested on his oars as he turned his head to look at the islet. His face lit up even more when he began rowing again.

The farmstead lay in the early morning sun, calm as could be. Why couldn't they be left in peace when they weren't bothering anybody? But someplace in the forest, deadly trackers they had never harmed were coming after them. The farmstead was off the beaten track, and the old owners were gone now. What did it matter if a few thralls whose owners had driven them off because of the famine settled down here?

Holme got mad again, thinking that if the men stayed with him, they might make it through a fight. The women, children, and the feeblest men could row over to the islet during the battle, but they would have to hurry. No one knew how soon the horsemen might get there.

Ausi greeted him with warm, troubled eyes, and he thought longingly about their past year of freedom at the settlement. Who knew if it would ever be that way again—sunny days with an impending harvest, peaceful nights in Ausi's arms?

But there wasn't time to think about such things. The people were awakened, and Holme briefly explained the situation to everybody. He had already given up the notion of fighting. There were just too many horsemen; not a single thrall would be left alive.

The boats set out soon with their first load. Holme stayed behind with the strongest men to detain the warriors if they arrived before the women and children were safe. But the boats came back and left with a new cargo, and still nothing moved at the edge of the forest. Some of the thralls hurriedly cut a boatload of the ripe grain and rowed across with it. Holme and his men came down the slope last, looking constantly toward the forest. It couldn't be long before the warriors would get there.

One of the thralls ran back to the building and returned with the little wooden god under his arm. Holme looked at him but didn't say anything. The men pulled back their legs so there'd be room for the god in the boat. Tiny ants crept in and out of the cracks furrowing his grinning wooden face. The farmstead and log landing moved farther and farther away, but everything remained quiet there. Maybe the warriors had given up and gone home.

After the chieftain and his warriors had pursued the bird's cry for a long time, the chieftain stopped at a well-worn path. Triumphantly he asked his men if they believed in Christ's sign now. He rode on, the horsemen following in single file, happy to abandon the rough ride in the woods with its low branches threatening to knock them off their horses. No one considered that, since they now had the sun in their faces, they had changed directions.

The chieftain quickened the pace, eager for the climax he was sure would be triumphant. The path began descending and soon they glimpsed an open field with water glittering below it. The field lay peaceful and quiet in the sun; a skinny pig, rooting alone by the shore, lifted its head and listened. The riders, their horses snorting, stopped at the edge of the forest and peered in bewilderment down at the settlement they had left at daybreak. Some of the men stifled their belly laughs in their beards.

The chieftain sat dumbfounded for a moment; then he assured them that Christ must have had some reason for bringing them back. He had doubtlessly seen some danger from heaven and had thus rescued them from it.

But the chieftain could see that the warriors were beginning to tire of the thankless hunt for thralls. It didn't matter much to them if the thralls got away; they'd much rather go back to town. The charred, wicked god no longer stood on the stone, so the blight would probably stop soon if he had sent it.

Inside the chieftain was bitter at Christ's having deceived him. He remembered the successes he had had when he was still a heathen. Maybe the powerful wooden battle god would help him one more time. Christ wouldn't like that, but if He wasn't going to help, what could He expect?

And so, mumbling in his beard, the chieftain promised rich gifts and sacrifices to the ancient god of his fathers if he'd deliver the thralls into his hands quickly. He conjured up the biggest image he could of the god, remembering he had been there long before Christ had. He surely knew the forest better and could give them the right directions.

The chieftain heard the warriors scorning Christ and His bird cry, but he kept quiet. He'd learn more about how to get help from Christ when a new priest showed up. For now, it couldn't hurt to be on the ancient gods' good side.

He ordered his men to dismount, rest, and get something to eat while they tried to decide what to do. They couldn't go home until they carried out the king's order. He tried to enrage the warriors by taunting them, telling them that thralls, women, and children had led them around by the nose for two days. They could burn the farmsteads but that wouldn't do anything. The thralls would just rebuild them again. They could destroy their grain, but the thralls wouldn't starve to death; they'd find some way to keep going. They had shown they could by robbing the Christians of grain.

The chieftain managed to provoke the warriors into giving it another try. The thralls couldn't have gone far. Many of the warriors approved of the chieftain's promise of gifts to the wooden gods if they would come to their aid.

Surely the thralls must have stayed near the farmsteads, probably waiting until the danger had passed to return.

Holme kept guard alone that night so the others could get some sleep. The thralls had spread out long beds of branches and grass under the densest trees they could find on the islet. Now they were all sleeping and the only sound to be heard was the lapping of the waves on the side of the islet facing into the wind.

The horsemen hadn't shown up all day. They might have gotten lost in the woods, but then again, it might be a trick. Or maybe they got tired and went home. A chieftain couldn't always get his warriors to do what he wanted.

Down on the shore in front of Holme stood the wooden god, looking across the water. He was supposed to be protecting the grainfields. A bundle of grain lay in front of him to remind him of his duties.

They could probably return after a few days. First Holme and a few of the men would check to see if the riders were waiting in the woods. If they had gone back to town, either he or someone else would find out if danger was on its way or if they'd be safe for a while.

He heard whispering from the people behind him. One of the younger couples had awakened and were playing with or caressing each other; he could hear the woman giggle. He got up and left quietly so as not to disturb them. Hearing them made him long for Ausi, but she was asleep beside Tora. It would be kind of fun anyway to see how she'd manage for them to be alone for a while. She always pretended it just happened. When she was younger she had always responded to him but she had never made the overtures as she did now.

When it became too cool to sit still, Holme walked around the islet a couple of times. The dew had settled on the grass and a cool gust of wind came in from the lake before the sun rose. A pair of seabirds swimming outside the reeds turned their triangular faces toward Holme before diving and surfacing farther away.

When Holme came back, the man who had been whispering with the woman raised his head and quietly offered to relieve him. The man couldn't sleep anyway. Holme accepted and they talked quietly about whether the warriors really had returned to town after failing in their hunt. Before going out on watch, the man covered the sleeping woman, and Holme lay down beside Ausi, who snuggled closer to him without waking.

Half asleep, he was aware of Ausi getting up and laying something over him; he let his eyes focus on the area around him but found no danger. He could see sunshine on green branches and could hear calm voices. Being awake for two nights weighted his eyelids heavily and he allowed himself to sleep a while longer. They could decide on the best thing to do when he woke up.

But the next time he woke someone was yelling his name. The call was an anxious one coming from the shore. He was alone in the sleeping area when he leaped up; the grass and twig beds lay there empty in the sunlight and shadow.

A number of voices were shouting from the shore now, and he was there in a flash. One of the boats was gone—it was tied at the log landing on the other side of the water. He saw three women running down the slope from the settlement toward the boat with horsemen galloping after them. The women would never make it to the boat. Holme looked hastily around, but neither Ausi nor Tora was anywhere to be seen.

As he untied the boat, anxious voices explained that the women had rowed over for the fishing gear. They needed fish and discovered that the gear was still at the landing. Although no one thought their pursuers were still around, the women had promised not to go up to the farmstead. But they had anyway and now they were all seeing the consequences.

The women were surrounded and disappeared among the horses. Before Holme shoved the boat out, a younger man hopped in with an ax in his hand. It was the one who had stood guard that morning. Holme looked toward the people on the shore again but couldn't see the man's wife. She was obviously the third one on the other side.

Holme knew there would be no sense in fighting this time. There were only two of them and arrows and spears might get them before they even reached land. The thrall told him that the riders had their weapons ready, but Holme rowed on without turning around. The people on the islet retreated into the distance, and he remembered they didn't have a boat. Maybe they could cross on logs and fetch the boats once the horsemen were gone.

The chieftain began admonishing Holme to give up even before he reached the landing, pointing out how hopeless it would be to resist. They had the dangerous man in a trap, and the chieftain felt glad and grateful to the wooden god who had helped them when Christ either wouldn't or couldn't. It might be a valuable thing to remember in the future.

The women had already been bound, and Ausi was in despair since she had never seen Holme give up without a fight before. She had put them in a bad situation again, even though she had meant well. Holme stepped out of the boat and stood before the warriors who approached cautiously, prepared for anything in spite of his being unarmed. The younger thrall had grabbed his ax but, looking at his captured woman, laid it hesitantly down and walked ashore behind Holme. The warriors tied them carefully without insults or scorn and their faces showed relief that the hunt was over.

The chieftain looked toward the islet and decided that the people over there could just as well stay for the time being. They couldn't escape and they weren't that important anyway. Holme and his family had been captured; that was the important thing. Their mission had been accomplished and the king would be pleased.

The chieftain ordered them to break camp. Hands bound, the prisoners followed along behind the last horses. The riders looked back frequently, having heard that Holme had knowledge exceeding other men's. They rode at a walk through the forest, and the thralls had no difficulty keeping up.

Ausi cried and chastised herself, but Holme was silent. He seemed deep in thought but not angry. Ausi knew he was planning their escape, and in her heart she called incessantly on Christ. If He could help them now, Holme would see and begin to believe in Him, too.

Toward evening, they reached the other farmstead. They were

thralls again and worse off now than ever before. The chieftain decided they would spend the night there and warned that the thralls weren't going to deceive them again. They'd keep watch two at a time and not let Holme out of their sight for a single moment.

The night was as peaceful and clear as the one before. Holme could see no way out for him and his family; two warriors sat armed and ready on the grass beside him. The women slept intermittently in their discomfort, crying and moaning in their sleep.

In the middle of the night, Holme heard a strange distant sound that seemed to come from the sea—an almost imperceptible murmur and muffled yell. The guards were talking quietly and didn't seem to notice. The sound lasted a moment then disappeared. Holme wondered what it could be. It came again at regular intervals, rising and falling. He had heard such sounds once from a fleet of big ships. They had many oars with one man at each oar, and the men shouted rhythmically so everyone would pull together. A large Viking fleet might be out there now. The wind was too calm to hoist a sail.

As the sound died away his thoughts returned. He knew they were headed for certain death; at least he and the younger thrall were. The women would probably be kept living in slavery. And yet he still wondered what the place where he had been both thrall and lord, and where he was now bound as a prisoner, would look like the next time he saw it. He was considered the most dangerous man in the land, even though all he had done was to try to help others. He had gotten grain for the starving thralls where there was grain to get, but that was regarded a criminal act. He was despised by the merchants for remaining with the thralls when he didn't have to. Had he forgotten his own slavery instead and begun living like the merchants, everything would have been all right and he would always have been the respected master smith. Ausi had wanted that more than once, but he had been born a thrall and as long as there were thralls anywhere, he had to be among them, working for their freedom. He had broken free himself, so he knew it could be done.

If the women hadn't decided to row across that morning, they all would have gotten away. But he didn't blame them; he shouldn't have slept so long. You couldn't give women responsibilities; he had found that out during the many years Ausi had been his wife. She would vacillate and do things she'd bitterly regret later. It couldn't be helped. She had been lured to the Christians several times and had accepted their baptism, but she never said a word anymore about Christ or his priests. She had reverted to her old self in the forest.

He thought, too, that if they did manage to escape and could gather the free thralls together again, they'd move so far north that no one could find them. They'd settle by some lake deep in the forest. They would break the ground and raise buildings, sow grain they'd take with them, forge weapons and tools. They'd erect walls around the farmstead, too, in case their enemies should come, after all.

He'd gather all the outlaws and the oppressed there; everyone would be free to earn a living. They'd never show themselves around the town again, where the population was dense. They'd have their own nation far away. Maybe they could still get some women to join them; most of the men in the forests would join. There might be so many women in those districts that each man could have his own.

He heard Ausi wake up and whisper something to Christ. If that comforted her, let her do it. Tora had been calm the whole day, looking as though she thought her father could save them whenever he wanted to, that it amused him to let the enemy be in control for a while. Toward evening, they'd probably be at the shore opposite the town. A hard day lay ahead of them.

Some black, powerful figures came into his thoughts, and he smiled in the darkness. He had friends in town who shouldn't be messed with. In one way or another the smiths would intervene once they heard he was a condemned prisoner.

Ausi edged closer to him, and the guards turned around suspiciously. After they had checked to make sure none of the straps was loose, they returned to their places. It had grown lighter and the couple could begin to see each other. Holme saw that all the anxiety had left Ausi's face, and she whispered to him that she wasn't afraid anymore. They would get help. And she rubbed against him affectionately.

She saw a rare smile light up the bitter features of his face, and she felt a strong surge of happiness at being his. Nothing would come between them, now that she knew Christ was with people like Holme. He was a lot like Christ; he too wanted everyone to be free and to live well. Christ must like him, even though he was heathen.

Early in the morning, the chieftain detailed some of the riders to follow behind with the thralls. He rode at the front with the bulk of the troop. They had been away longer than he had thought they would be, and he was impatient to get home and report to the king. A stately man with a short-clipped beard was put in charge of the small detail. The chieftain reminded him how important it was for the prisoners to be closely watched. If they got away, they'd both suffer for it.

Then the chieftain disappeared into the forest with most of the warriors, and those left behind prepared to break camp. Ausi looked at the new leader, wondering, half afraid, who he was. His gaze and build seemed familiar. He looked back at her a moment and it came to her. It was Geire, the man who had raped her. He had grown thin, the bridge of his nose was caved in, and he had cut his beard, but it was still him.

At first, she thought of saying something to Holme, who surely wouldn't recognize him. She also thought of telling him about the rape but restrained herself; it was so hard for Holme anyway. If he got angry enough, he might break loose and attack the men, but there were several of them and they were armed—they'd cut him down. If they were going to die—Holme, she, and Tora—it was best to keep quiet about what had happened. If they managed to escape, she could tell Holme about it later when he was free and could take revenge.

Geire's gaze, which before had been open and resolute, now seemed grave and treacherous. There was also something in it that made her remember the battle on the floor in front of the door. Ausi sensed that he would rape her again if he got the chance. But Holme was there and would protect her even if he was tied up. At the right time, Christ would allow Holme to do whatever was best for all of them.

Six riders would escort them to town, and Ausi could see that Holme's face was brighter than it had been the day before. Holme could take six men if he were free and had a weapon. Maybe during the day his chance would come.

The thralls were allowed to have their legs untied, and they staggered among the horses a while before the journey began. Two men rode at the front with the younger thrall and his woman; then came three others with Holme, Ausi, and Tora tied behind the horses. Geire rode last so he could watch all of them constantly.

Back in town, Geire, hearing that Holme and his thralls would be tracked down and captured, had immediately sought the chieftain out to ask permission to go along. One of the two farmsteads the thralls had taken over belonged to him and the other to his sister. When the chieftain heard that, he decided it might be a good idea to have a warrior along who both knew the area and hated Holme and the thralls.

It was, in fact, because of Geire that they had finally managed to capture Holme and the others. He had ridden off to his farmstead by himself and discovered the thralls fleeing to the islet. It had then only been a matter of setting up an ambush for them since the riders didn't have boats to get to the islet.

The chieftain had no qualms about leaving the prisoners in Geire's custody after he'd heard the things he had against Holme. But despite everything, Holme was a known and, in his way, a respected man; it wouldn't go over well to kill him like a dog in the woods as Geire wanted. Undoubtedly, the king wanted to make him responsible for the blight, and so he would also want to mete out his punishment himself. The wife and daughter would surely be returned to their former owner once Holme was dead.

Geire was riding behind the prisoners and was, on the whole, satisfied. Over a year ago, the thralls had beaten him to the ground with their sticks, but he had begun to settle accounts.

Never in all his life had he imagined that someday he would have to join an army against thralls. He had always considered them necessities on a farmstead, nothing you had to deal with like ordinary people. But the smith walking in front of him had made himself a free man and had given many others the notion that they too could be free to fend for themselves. It was dangerous to let such a thought spread. Slaves far outnumbered freemen, and if they got hold of weapons, things could end disastrously.

However, with Holme captured, the danger was past. Geire's sister would get Ausi and the daughter back as thralls, as was only right. And then everyone could sleep without worrying about hearing the resounding blow of a sledgehammer on the door at night.

The thralls in front of him had had their arms freed so they could move faster. They were secured only with leather straps around their waists, but the straps were so strong that ten smiths couldn't break them. The women had taken off their jackets and were walking with their shoulders bare. It was a clear, warm autumn day, and they had to trudge through dense thickets.

That whole year, Geire had been unable to forget the thrall woman he had raped on the floor. She walked ahead of him now; he could see her bare shoulders and the battle raged in his memory—her alabaster body, struggling and panting; the final surrender and his victory. It was shameful that his sister had awakened and pinned her arms, but at the time all he'd been able to do was accept the help.

Geire didn't just want to rape her again; he wanted to live with the woman. The thought that she might someday come to him of her own free will seemed to him an idea worth living and striving for. Her husband was going to die; someday, after a little time had passed, he might be able to get along with her all right. Svein could have the daughter; it was small recompense for the deformity her father had bestowed upon him.

Sometimes he believed that Ausi had cast a spell on him to avenge the rape. Before, he had given no thought to women after his farmstead had burned. There had been a woman thrall there he had visited regularly. But this last year he had had no peace. He had tried others, only to realize an even stronger desire for the woman walking before him now with supple, fluid hips.

At midday, Geire decided they would stop and rest. They were in a little glade with mixed forest around it. The horses began grazing, and the thralls sat down behind them, sliding themselves along behind whenever the horses moved and made the straps too tight.

Geire had come to a decision during the last hour. He felt shame, but his lust was too intense and he couldn't help it. Softly he talked with the other men and their eyes began twinkling and roving around. They could have the young girl and the thrall woman; Holme's wife he reserved for himself. No one would know; besides, no one would care. Both men were going to die, and the women would return to slavery.

Quivering with excitement, the warriors approached the thralls and suddenly threw themselves on the men, who still didn't quite grasp what was happening. They managed to throw a strap around Holme's wrists and pull it tight. The young thrall was tied the same way, and then all the warriors worked together tying their legs with another strap. Having done that, they freed the women from the horses.

The thralls finally understood what the men were up to. The women struggled, kicking and biting as they were dragged toward the edge of the forest by the panting men. Holme and the thrall rolled on the ground, roaring and yanking on the straps. The horses, getting restless, neighed and tossed their heads.

Hearing his daughter's screams from the bushes, Holme pulled his legs up with a powerful yank and caught the strap with his bound hands. With a violent jerk, he snapped the strap and leaped to his feet. The horses spooked, broke loose, and took off toward the woods. Holme threw his body backward with all his might and the straps tying him to the horse snapped, too. But his friend, dragged bouncing along behind his horse, disappeared into the brush.

His hands still tied, Holme ran toward the fighting and scream-ing. He met one of the men who had come out to see what was dis-turbing the horses. The man stared at Holme and reached for his weapon, but Holme gave him a tremendous kick. He fell to the ground and lay there while the others, letting go of the women, rushed over. A quick glance assured Holme that all three women remained untouched.

But five men surrounded him with weapons drawn while he was alone with his hands tied. Geire soon calmed down and stopped the others from cutting the prisoner down. He must be handed over to the chieftain alive, or it could mean their lives too. As he watched the women getting up triumphantly and rearrang-ing their clothes, he shot a dark, hate-filled look at Holme. The smith had upset his plans this time, too, but never again.

Geire guarded the prisoners himself while the others searched for the horses snorting nearby. They found them soon enough and the bloody, torn thrall came stumbling along behind them af-ter they had untied his legs. His woman cried out with joy, then an-swered the question in his eyes, explaining eagerly that nothing had happened to her or the others. Holme, who still hadn't caught his breath, was surprised and relieved to see that the thrall was still alive in spite of being dragged behind the horse. He was glaring with hatred at the horsemen as he spit out dirt and grass.

But the man Holme had kicked in the stomach wasn't moving. The others turned him over and tried to sit him up, but blood was running down his beard and he fell limply to the ground. Geire decided they should rest a while longer so he'd have a chance to come to. Already he regretted what had just happened and wished somehow it could be undone. He turned away from the hatred and disdain in the thralls' eyes. After this, he would never be able to woo Ausi once she was alone and independent.

It was midday and the group of people, so recently violent, now was quiet and still. The leaves of the young aspen trees rustled slowly, and the dragonflies flew back and forth over the clearing with a slow beating of wings. The young thrall woman tore chunks of moss and wiped the blood from her man's face and hands.

Holme's legs were still free, and he sat between Ausi and Tora. He was thinking about the things that had just happened, how close they had come to freedom. If his hands had been free, he would have taken on those five men. But the day wasn't over yet. He thought with distaste of the town, and something from the fathomless forests tugged at him with a magnetic force.

Again Holme heard the strange sound he had heard the night before, barely audible but rhythmic, sometimes more distinct, then dying completely away. He glanced around, but none of the others appeared to hear anything.

He knew approximately how far it was to town; they had long stretches of the lake to the west of them. The sound came from there. An almost inaudible, yet roaring and rhythmical, yell. It seemed to come from the very sunshine and silence themselves. Perhaps it was from the land beyond the dead, and that was why he alone heard it. That didn't scare him, but he was uneasy at the thought of what they would do to Ausi and Tora when he was gone. He had just had a glimpse of what they could expect.

He pushed the thoughts aside and listened again. He heard the sound retreating farther to the west then dying away in the rustling of the aspen leaves. The still-motionless man lay at the foot of the trees, his cheeks ashen beneath his beard.

It was a quiet, angry Geire who gave the order to break camp a short time later. Finally he had realized that the man was dead, so they tied him securely onto his horse. He hung across the saddle, blood dripping on the ground as the horse walked.

For the moment, Geire's lust for the woman had been dampened by the violent and unpredictable events, and he was thinking that the most important thing now was to complete their mission. Geire began to believe himself that Holme was in league with the powers beyond, and it would be a relief to leave him in the chieftain's hands. Geire examined the straps Holme had ripped apart, convinced that no ordinary human being could have done that. Not five ordinary men. And he had never heard of a single kick being enough to kill a man without his even making a sound.

But he still felt bitter disappointment at not getting a chance to rape the woman. Everything had been so well planned; none of them had thought anything could stop them. The opportunity would come round again after Holme's death, though, and then there'd be no one who'd be able to stop him. He could still sense the smell of leaves and damp moss from the ground where he'd wrestled briefly with Ausi. Then he had heard the horses breaking loose and the girl screaming for her father. That despairing shriek had only further incited Holme to violence. It would have served Holme right to have to lie there, tied up, hearing everything, but he had won again, for the last time.

Geire saw the fear and anger in the other men's eyes whenever they turned toward Holme. What was it about him that was so ominous and threatening, in spite of his customary silence? Geire scrutinized him closely for the first time. He was taller than he looked; his shoulders were broad and full, his hands large and well-formed. But there was something else; there were many men who looked like they'd be just as strong. He couldn't pinpoint it exactly, but no one could meet Holme and not be impressed. You had to be either his enemy or his friend. But his only friends were among the thralls, even though freemen had treated him as their equal. And he still held his head high, thinking himself as good as anyone else. It was high time that such a mysterious being got his just punishment—death.

They'd have to travel faster now to arrive on time. The prisoners had the straps tied around their waists again, but their arms had been left free so they could run behind the horses. They'd soon reach a wider road that was bumpy and winding but at least it wouldn't have boulders and bushes to slow them down.

Embittered, Geire sat on his horse behind the prisoners. The man tied up in front of him might have frustrated his plans, but Geire was the leader and would have some kind of revenge while he still could. He could at least run the obstinancy out of the prisoners by nightfall. Both thralls had pretended they were freemen, and their women considered themselves too good to be taken by free warriors.

When they emerged onto the road, Geire told the his men what he had in mind and they agreed at once. The thralls had won in the glade back there, but now they'd teach them.

Holme had already guessed what was coming, and his threatening, disdainful look provoked Geire even more. From his position behind the prisoners, he could soon see them start running as the straps began tightening around their waists. The women lifted their skirts with one hand, and he could see their bare legs. That intensified his excitement, and he yelled to the riders to go faster. In the meantime, he wondered what had come over him, a quiet, good-tempered warrior and farmer. That woman had probably cast a spell on him so he was no longer himself.

The legs in front of him moved faster and faster, and the thralls began panting more and more heavily. He saw Holme turn his head and look first at his wife and then at his daughter to see how long they could hold out. Suddenly Ausi tripped, but before she could fall, Holme's arm shot out and grabbed her. He ran on as she clung panting to his arm. Grudgingly, Geire marveled again at the smith's strength and quickness, which had to exceed that of any normal man.

Holme soon got his wife back on her feet again and supported her until she could follow along. At the same time he snatched up his daughter with the other arm, and she flung her arms around his neck. As far back as Geire was he could hear the thralls' wheezing, so finally he ordered the riders to slow to a walk. Maybe the thralls had mellowed by now.

Holme put Tora down and shot a look back at Geire. Holme's face was swollen and shiny with the sweat running down it. Geire was not a timid man, but it was clear to him that Holme's impending death would be his own salvation. The smith before him was not to be taken lightly. His enemies would forever be in mortal danger. The fact remained that even though Holme had been tied up during the whole journey, a dead warrior dangled across Geire's horse.

But they'd be in town before nightfall. Though Geire had failed with the woman in the woods, soon no one would be able to stop him from doing whatever he pleased with her and her daughter.

The third time, Holme wasn't the only one who heard the strange, rhythmical sounds. From deep in the woods they could hear the sounds as they neared the landing and Geire called for silence: the shout of multitudes blended with the distinct roar of churning water. Geire galloped up a hill near the road but couldn't see anything. The eerie sounds created an atmosphere of their own, but for Geire it was nothing new. The wind was completely down and he realized that many large battleships had come out onto the lake. What they heard was the rhythmical yell of the oarsmen rowing in unison; the churning water came from the prows and the plunging oars.

Soon it was clear to Holme, too, where the sound was coming from. They had had a long way to go in the silent night and peaceful day, but now only a rim of forest stood between them and the town. Geire ordered them to approach cautiously so they could take a look without being discovered from the lake. They could see hoofprints the whole way where the road passed through swampy areas.

Even before they reached the forest's edge, they could catch glimpses of the cheery colors among the trees. Geire ordered the riders to stop, and they watched a large Viking fleet rowing slowly by on the lake. The shout sounded hard and rhythmic and hundredfold. The long oars glistened in the evening sunlight as the water ran off them, and the golden dragons, their red maws gaping widely toward the town, glared rigidly at it.

Geire and his men stared in astonishment and disappointment at the ships, but Holme once again contemplated escape. The chieftain and the king had something else to think about now. He could see people swarming into the harbor, and a narrow file of people streaming toward the fortress. Enemies were on their way to plunder and burn.

Geire conferred with his men a moment, then decided to leave the horses on the mainland. The oarsman was nowhere to be seen and the ferry was on the other side, but a few small boats were at the shore. They might have time to get over and into the town before it was surrounded. Surely the dragon ships wouldn't bother chasing the small boats when they were so close to the town.

Holme didn't want to jeopardize his and his family's lives by starting a fight on the shore. It would be better to cross peacefully to the other side. In the great confusion that would engulf the town a better opportunity for escape might come along.

People came running from farmsteads to the shore to watch the

Vikings. The owners of the small boats stood there guarding them, but by threatening the chieftain's disfavor, Geire finally managed to borrow two of the boats. The horses had to be left as collateral.

When they lifted the dead man from his horse to put him into a boat, they found that his body had stiffened in the shape of a bow. They couldn't straighten him out so had to drape him over the prow, exchanging vexed words about his having to walk doubled over through the land of the dead. It wouldn't be easy for him to use his weapons or get around.

Away from shore, they could see the harbor guards on the run, trying to organize the defense; frenetic horn blasts sailed across the water. But not a group of warriors was ready for battle, and people kept fleeing to the fortress. On the nearby lookout hill stood a group of men looking down at the advancing enemy. Boats of all sizes had taken off from shore, but a couple of the dragons broke out of the fleet and would soon block their path to the coves and all their hiding places. The rest of the fleet headed straight for the harbor, but the shout of the oarsmen had fallen silent and the boats were changing formation as they approached.

Geire and his men rowed with their prisoners between the fleeing and the pursuing boats. Cold wakes from the big ships came rolling into them, rocking them violently, and they could see long rows of shields along the sides of the ships. But no one would bother chasing two little boats from the mainland. The ones from town, on the other hand, would have valuables on board.

They managed to reach the jutting edge of land and get ashore out of sight of the ships. The younger thrall looked questioningly at Holme and signaled with his wounded head; he thought they should make their move, even though their hands were still tied, but Holme shook his head. He knew better than to think he could kick to death five men who were armed and wary of him. There'd be better opportunities. They could hear the tumult from the lake but couldn't see anything from where they stood. The dragons had probably caught their prey.

With this new situation threatening ruin for the whole town, the warriors forgot that the thralls were dangerous, too. They dragged them hurriedly along, scarcely looking back at all. They were afraid they might not make it to the fortress before the enemy landed and laid siege to it. It wouldn't be a good idea to be outside once that happened. No one knew what the advancing enemy would do—demand ransom from the town and sail off, or plunder and burn and kill everything in their path.

Holme knew there'd be no battle. Too many enemy warriors were arriving and there didn't seem to be anyone to stop them in the harbor. Perhaps the king and most of his men were gone. In that case the men on the lookout hill might be the chieftain and the warriors who had been with him on the thrall hunt, and another hunt would soon begin.

The warriors and thralls jogged through the grove and across the meadow. The prisoners didn't resist so the straps dangled loose all the way. Soon they were below the hill, looking up at the warriors on the top, who quickly turned toward the strange little group that had just broken out of the forest. When the group reached the top, the chieftain's face was deeply troubled, and he barely listened to Geire's report of the journey. He said the king was gone; they were just too few of them to fight, but they'd lock themselves in the fortress and defend themselves as long as they could. Maybe Christ would come to their aid.

From the hill, Holme could see that many people were hurrying toward the forest, not the fortress, and he thought bitterly to himself that they were undoubtedly the thralls who weren't allowed to take up valuable space and therefore had to seek shelter wherever they could find it. A few men were walking toward the harbor to meet the enemy. Holme had known for a long time that some young thralls would go over to the enemy in order to get new lords in another land. But they might just as easily be cut down or driven off. So they walked hesitantly, always on the alert.

The chieftain considered a moment what to do with the prisoners. He would have liked to kill the men and drive off the women, but the king's order was still in effect, so he finally decided to take them into the fortress. The men would have to be kept under constant guard, but the women could help with the work if need be.

As he was being led into the fortress, Holme saw the enemy breaking through the barriers in the harbor and swarming onto shore. The town defenders came running toward the fortress in the mounting dusk.

The fortress was teeming with people of all ages. Many of them had spread their animal skins and clothes on the ground for their children and had set their store chests down beside them. Some had ponderous, ironclad chests that weighed more than a man; others had simple wooden ones. The richest merchants and their wives wore expensive clothes with gold and pearls hanging down the arms.

A lot of people recognized Holme in the dim light, and a surprised murmur arose as the prisoners were brought forward. Some of the townspeople grumbled out loud about thralls and outlaws taking up precious space. But other voices anxiously countered that it was all the same since they'd probably all fall victim to the enemies' weapons, and all the women would be enslaved. Everywhere, women and children were moaning and crying.

Holme listened for the smiths' voices, but couldn't hear them anywhere. It would hardly have been possible to keep them out of the fortress if they had wanted to come in. His hands were still bound, and although the women had been untied, they were forbidden to move freely within the fortress. They rubbed their swollen wrists and tried in any way they could to make things easier for their men. All the while, they kept staring at the expensively dressed women glittering in the dim light.

It was nearly dark when the gate opened for one last group of men. Holme didn't see them, but he couldn't mistake their voices. They reported that the enemy had the whole town in their hands now and would soon reach the fortress. But they hadn't killed anyone or burned any buildings.

The smiths' news quickened the atmosphere in the fortress, and many of the people began to hope they'd escape with their lives. The warriors had taken up positions along the wall, ready to fight if the enemy suddenly stormed the fortress. But it was more likely that they would wait for daylight so the defenders couldn't see them outlined against the sky as they rushed up the slope.

The smiths moved to the far side of the fortress and their voices were lost in the noise. Holme and Ausi talked softly about how surprised the smiths would be when dawn broke and they could all see each other. The guards weren't staying so close anymore, probably figuring that there were enough guards outside the fortress. No one in his right mind would want to leave the protection of the fortress to be cut down.

They finally lay down to try to sleep. It had been a rough, exhausting day, but they hadn't been hurt. They were still alive, and Ausi was convinced that Christ had sent the enemies for their deliverance. The chieftain was a baptized Christian, but enemies were still threatening his town and himself—proof that his wasn't the real Christ.

The noise died away as night fell, replaced occasionally by heavy breathing and snores. Ausi lay on her back, watching the dark clouds above her. A star sparkled through now and then where the clouds thinned out or dispersed. Once a bright circle of stars took shape over her face. It remained fixed for a moment, and she thought that Christ had parted the clouds to see what was happening to His wards. She was filled with joy and began guessing how He was going to save them.

Holme and Tora were asleep next to Ausi. She thought how she and her daughter had been rescued in the forest and was grateful. The men had planned to rape Tora, a mere child who had never even looked at a man. But they had underestimated Holme; though he was bound hand and foot, he had struggled to her aid and saved all three women from the rapists. A few minutes later and it would have been too late. Holme had kicked one rapist to death, the one who now lay bent double at the shore. They hadn't had time to carry him with them. They had laid his weapon beside him, thrown some branches over him, and said they'd be back after the battle.

She could hear the chieftain's voice in the distance as he conferred with the town leaders. They speculated about how big a ransom they would have to pay to keep life and town intact. They also considered the gods and what they should sacrifice to them. The chieftain raised his voice when he affirmed that only Christ could help them now and that this would never have happened if everyone had lived a good Christian life like he did.

In the middle of the night fresh warriors relieved those standing guard. The ones going off duty said that the fortress had been surrounded since dusk. They had heard muffled voices and rattling weapons. The enemy would probably attack at daybreak.

People would wake up now and then, yawn, and try to keep their voices calm when they spoke. Occasionally a baby would whimper or someone would call out in his sleep. The young thrall and his woman slept in a close embrace near Ausi.

After midnight the whistling wind rose among the trees around the fortress and Ausi felt raindrops on her face. She put her own garment over Holme and Tora, then lay down herself without any covering. Joyfully she felt how cold and wet she was getting. She had finally found something she could do for them. But the rain shower got heavier and soon water was running under the sleeping people. Holme woke up first, and those near them soon started moving and getting up. A roof jutted out from inside the fortress wall, so they woke Tora and hurried there for shelter.

After the rain, the ground was too wet to lie on. Everyone walked around miserably, trying to keep warm. The thralls' guards were walking around too, and no one noticed in the darkness that two of the thralls had their hands tied. Holme had hoped that during the night they might get a knife or something to cut the straps with, but they hadn't been able to yet. He also realized that the tense, irritable crowd would welcome a chance to attack a couple of bound thralls. At dawn he'd probably see the smiths and get free. Then no matter what happened, at least they wouldn't die with their hands tied, and with his hands free, Holme wouldn't die alone.

The straps had cut into their wrists until their arms went numb. The women rubbed and caressed them to ease the pain and to show their affection. But Tora still looked at her father in bewilderment; she couldn't believe he was going along with all this. When he had kicked the man to death in the forest, she had laughed delightedly but nothing had changed. But since he was going along with everything, he must be waiting for something. He was the strongest man of all.

The gray light of dawn began to spread in the east over the lake, and inside the fortress they were finally able to see. A number of people began loosening their clothes and walking toward a fenced-off area. The chieftain climbed up on the barricade to survey the surrounding enemy. Everyone inside the fortress could hear them; they were talking loudly and occasionally laughing. They probably had no respect for their victims. The chieftain, who had traveled widely and could tell where they came from by their speech, told his men they were Danes and that it was a good sign they hadn't attacked yet. Maybe they'd be satisfied with a ransom.

The smiths shook their heads in disbelief when a man told them that Holme was a prisoner in the fortress. He had been gone a long time, and they hadn't heard anything about his coming back. And he wasn't easy to capture and hold prisoner.

But the man persisted, and the smiths finally went searching among the wet, miserable crowd. Holme saw them coming, and the surprised smiths soon surrounded the prisoners. Without a word the oldest smith drew his knife and cut the straps, first Holme's and then the younger thrall's. Both men gratefully stretched their arms, smiling with relief.

The smiths' surprise turned quickly to happiness at the reunion. A number of the wealthy merchant families glared at the smiths and thralls who belonged in the forest, not taking up room here. Ever since Holme had come to town, the smiths and craftsmen had been insubordinate and too sure of themselves. But that wasn't all—Holme had even managed to make ordinary thralls think they were just as good as freemen. Look at them standing there now, talking openly and happily as if they were the most important people in town.

There were three people who regarded them with even greater disdain. Geire had found his sister and Svein, who were glad to hear that Holme was a prisoner and would soon die. The chieftain's wife would get Ausi and Tora back again—it was her due. She had already given her brother permission to do whatever he wanted to with Ausi. And she was pleased to see that Svein had prowled like an aroused animal all night after discovering that the girl was in the fortress.

As soon as day broke they had started looking for the thralls so they could gloat over their misery. But the smiths were there first and the prisoners were free. Once again the chieftain's wife had to endure seeing Ausi as beautiful as ever, unaffected by all she'd been through. Tora was almost grown, and though she wasn't beautiful, she still caught your eye. She'd probably become a sorcerer like her father.

She gleefully noticed that Holme's hair was graying at the temples and that his face had grown thin. His cheekbones were more prominent than before and his eyes deeper set. He'd be dead soon and then she would get even with the slave woman and her daughter. It had been a long time since she had offered silver to the wooden god in order to get hold of them, but he had finally lived up to his part of the bargain.

Ausi's eyes caught the spiteful look in those of her former owner and she moved a few steps closer to Holme even though the smiths stood protectively in a ring around them. She knew what was in store for her and Tora if those three ever got their hands on them again. Geire was looking angrily at the smiths but no doubt realized how hard they would be to handle. She recognized Svein by the steely way his eyes stared at Tora, seldom blinking. He had grown as tall as Geire and was armed like a warrior. She hoped he would never get his hands on Tora.

Suddenly a loud horn blast came from outside the fortress, bringing immediate silence inside. A clear voice in their own tongue warned them that the enemy was strong enough to storm the fortress and kill everyone in it. They could raze the town, too, if they wanted. They would spare the town, though, since their chieftain had once been king in this land but had been driven away. He wanted to make peace with his former people despite the indignity he had suffered.[15]

When the townspeople heard the former king's name, they looked at each other and remembered. He was a man of his word, but he had been driven away for trying to force his own will above that of the people at the assembly. Now, he was back with an army.

The voice spoke again, promising that those inside would be allowed to live and keep their town but for a price. And the voice stopped when it told them how big the price would be. They demanded a quick answer; otherwise they would attack.

The chieftain gathered the merchants around him, and a lively exchange began. Everyone seemed relieved; they'd be left alive and the ransom wasn't as much as they had feared. Holme watched this chain of events uneasily. If the enemy withdrew, the danger for them was just as great as before. He and the smiths couldn't hope to fight the whole town even if the smiths were fully armed.

When the meeting was over, the chieftain stepped up on the rampart so that his gray head could be seen from every direction.

15. The king's name, according to Rimbert (*Anskar*, chapter 19, p. 65), is Anoundus, and the raid described on the following pages occurred after Gautbert's replacement, Ardgar, arrived in Sweden (i.e., seven years later, not one year).

He answered that, though it was a great burden, they would pay the ransom in silver demanded of them. Even as he spoke, the silver was being measured into a chest and would be set outside one of the gates. He hoped that the enemy wouldn't change their minds and would sail away as promised.

From where they stood, the prisoners could see the chieftain taking silver from the merchants and weighing it before putting it in the chest. There were masses of tiny white coins, long silver bars, and rings of all sizes. Even the poor had to contribute what they could to ransom their lives. The sum demanded was finally in the chest, and the chieftain had it dragged to one of the gates. Warriors were ordered to stand on both sides of the gate with swords drawn in case anyone tried sneaking into the fortress.

Once the gate was closed again, the atmosphere among the people was buoyant. They sighed in relief and began thinking about their everyday concerns again. All they had to do was wait until the enemy sailed away and then they could go back to town.

They gathered round the prisoners, looking at them with curiosity or malice while they repeated to each other the crimes the thralls had committed. Geire took this opportunity to approach the chieftain and remind him about the prisoners. He asked that his sister be permitted to take Ausi and Tora with her—as had been decided at the assembly—when she left the fortress. Soon Holme saw the chieftain approaching, surrounded by merchants and warriors. They stopped in front of the group of thralls and silent smiths, who stood waiting to one side.

The chieftain spoke and reminded everybody about Holme's past, how he had escaped from his owners and passed himself off as a freeman in town. How he then plundered the Christians' storehouse and handed out the grain to his fellow thralls while the rest of the towns' populace lived on the brink of starvation. Then he described the attack on the Christian church and the murder of the priest. Holme had been condemned as an outlaw long ago, but time after time he had returned to town. No one until now had managed to strike him down, but his time had come.

The chieftain talked, too, about the charred god on the rock far away in the forest. Holme had used his sorcery to make the god spread the blight over the grain: everyone knew that. Many people had starved to death and still more might starve during the winter. The chieftain concluded by telling of the thrall hunt and the capture. As proof that all he said was true, he pointed out that the grain at the thrall farmsteads was free from the blight that was ravaging everywhere else.

Ausi listened to the chieftain's speech more and more anxiously, wondering how all the good Holme had done could be construed as a criminal outrage. If a thrall had told the story, the truth would have come to light. He would have told how Holme had fixed his tools for nothing, had taken him into his house and given him food and drink, had risked his own life and liberty to obtain food for the thralls when they were near death from hunger, and had forgotten himself. He had shared their troubles and in the end had tried to make them free and happy. If Holme was a criminal, so was Christ, who also went around helping the poor and down-trodden. And now they were going to kill Holme for the good he had done.

Holme's face was unaffected by the chieftain's story, but the smiths looked surprised and troubled. They had known Holme for many years, but they couldn't deny that he had done what the chieftain accused him of. Even so, they had no intention of letting him be killed in front of their eyes. He had been good to them and fair; when the time came they'd be on his side.

However, they soon heard the chieftain say that the prisoners would be held in safekeeping until the king returned. He'd stand judge over them himself. The smiths calmed down, resolved not to sit idly by in the meantime. Sledgehammers and axes could sink into most doors.

Before the chieftain could issue his final order, the lookout shouted to him and he climbed back up on the barricade. The sun had come up and was shining on his gray hair and horned helmet.[16] Down in the meadow between the town and the fortress the enemy was crowded around the silver chest, and a roar of agitated voices was rising. The chieftain could see that they didn't think there was enough ransom. A huge warrior kicked the chest in disdain and looked around defiantly.

The chieftain realized they had celebrated too soon; the danger still hadn't passed. The invaders probably hadn't appreciated their chieftain asking for so little from so rich a town. The noise grew louder, and the chieftain came down to talk with his closest advisors. The crowd surrounding the prisoners thinned out again with the advent of the bad news, and everyone crowded around the chieftain, terror on their faces. A number of them loudly promised their gods great gifts and sacrifices if they would help them out of this new peril.

But the chieftain had gone back to Christ even though the wooden god had done him a good turn when he was hunting thralls in the forest. He spoke now, advising the merchants to

16. The popular notion that Vikings wore horned helmets cannot be supported by archeological evidence, all of which suggests that the Viking helmet was conical. Horned helmets may have been worn for ceremonial purposes during the Bronze Age and pre-Viking period, but the evidence for that is slight as well. See James Graham-Campbell, *The Viking World* (New Haven: Ticknor & Fields, 1980), p. 24, and Almgren, *The Viking*, p. 221.

promise Christ their gifts because the wooden gods had only deceived them. The ransom was lost, and it looked as if the enemy would plunder, burn, and kill despite their promise to sail away. The chieftains probably couldn't control the warriors.

The chieftain graphically described how they would storm the fortress, kill all the men, and rape or steal the women. All because his people didn't believe in Christ. It did not occur to him that the same fate would befall him.

He spoke in an ominous voice, and the merchants began turning hesitantly away from the image of the battle god that stood in the fortress to put their fate into the chieftain's hands. He finally relented and turned his face upward to put their case before Christ. He pointed out that he had been a good Christian from the start, emphasizing the services he had done the priests. He finished by listing the gifts the merchants were willing to give; in addition, the people wouldn't eat meat for a prescribed number of days.

The people around him watched timidly and attentively, and many of them peered up into the swirling white clouds, searching for the new god's face. The noise from the enemy mounted, threatening to crash down from the sky onto the beleaguered fortress.

The thralls left on the islet watched with sorrow and anger as the horsemen captured Holme, the young thrall, and the women. When they had disappeared into the forest and everything was quiet, the thralls felt like a flock of abandoned children. What would they do without Holme?

They knew their pursuers wanted Holme, not them, but the boats were at the opposite shore, too far away to swim. Their provisions would give out soon, and the wild berries wouldn't last for long. They could see their barley fields across the water—large patches of gold beside the gray buildings. The grain was ready to be harvested; it would fall from the stalks soon and lie useless on the ground.

The men started chopping down trees the same day. They stripped the trunks and dragged them to shore, made ropes out of everybody's clothes, and tied the logs together into a raft. By evening it was in the water, and it could hold about half of them. They had split big pieces of wood for oars.

The clumsy raft inched across the still water while a group of thralls sat waiting mutely on the islet. Occasionally they heard a strange, rhythmical sound that seemed to come from an endless distance, a sound no one had ever heard before. It floated across the water from where the lake opened into the sea. The women shivered, fearing sorcery and bad omens. What could it mean? Maybe the riders were still in the woods and would attack the men once they got across.

When the raft bumped into the landing, one of the younger men hopped up on shore while the others shoved off again to safety. They still suspected a trap. The younger man was single, without wife and child, and he had volunteered to go ashore and reconnoiter. He could run away from the riders and hide in the woods. And why would they want to catch him anyway? He couldn't possibly be worth more than Holme.

The other men agreed to let him have his way. They watched him as he walked past the grainfield; he tore off an ear, rubbed it between his hands, and blew away the bran before stuffing the grain in his mouth. He was probably trying to show how calm he was. He circled the building to see if anyone was hiding there. Finally he ventured into the forest, and the men could hear him heaping scorn and defiance on the riders. But there was no response, and he soon came back down the slope. The others went ashore too, except for those going back for the rest of the thralls.

By midnight everyone was across, and the hoofprints were still visible in the mire on the shore. It was warmer at the forest's edge than on the islet, where the wind never really stopped blowing. The smell of ripe barley permeated the night, and the damp grass felt cool against their ankles. But Holme was gone, and none of them felt safe there anymore even though it had been their home for a year. A couple of the men stood guard outside while the others went inside to try to get some sleep.

One of the women complained bitterly about the way life had been since they gained their freedom. It had been good, but what would it be like now? No peace, night or day; who could stand that? She was sorry she hadn't stayed in town as a thrall. Her mistress might have beaten her black and blue when she was in a bad mood, but that was still better than life on the run in the woods. They could never return to town and see people; they could never even get any new clothes.

The others sitting or lying on the benches and floor began to mull over what she had said, and soon they were murmuring in the corners. But in the end, it was only the complaining woman who had spoken who really wanted to go back to slavery. The rest searched for the right words to express their feelings, but it was hard. Had Holme heard them, he would have been glad that the thralls had freedom lodged so deeply in their hearts after just one year. They would never forget it and would tell the story of their year of freedom as long as they lived.

One of the older men reminded them what Holme had said, that everyone should be free and live their lives the way they wanted to. In a weak but steady voice he asked, weren't thralls as strong as freemen and just as skillful workers and warriors? Didn't

a thrall hurt as much when he was beaten and suffering as a freeman did? Weren't slave women just as beautiful as freewomen?
Oh, the freemen obviously thought so, too, since they always took
the most beautiful slave women by fair means or foul, he concluded bitterly and scornfully.

But the woman didn't back down; instead, she asked when
they'd be able to enjoy their freedom if they were never left alone.
When would they dare walk the roads and paths as other people
did? Where would they get the goods they needed when they
couldn't barter with and buy things from anybody? They could
never show themselves at the great sacrificial feasts. The freemen
would kill them if they did, so they'd have to hide in the woods.
And so would their children. What good would their freedom be
then? the woman demanded bitterly, and her question was answered with a heavy silence. Most of them thought she was right;
looked at from her point of view, freedom was more burdensome
and dangerous than anything else could be.

The woman sat triumphantly in the darkness and dared the
older man to respond. He finally said that he wasn't the one who
had discovered freedom and given it to them; Holme was and he
probably would have been able to answer her. Hadn't they lived
well during the past year? And when Holme came back he'd probably know how to get even with the enemy again. He might mar-
shal all the thralls in the land together, mount an army against the
freemen, and make them all slaves. But no, that's not how it would
be; thralls shouldn't exist at all. Better just to kill the freemen.

The thrall's thoughts were leading him nowhere, and he soon
tired of the effort. Holme would have all the answers for everything when he returned. If they could only stay at the farmsteads,
they'd have nothing to complain about. The old man told the
woman that and then lay back down to sleep hoping that Holme

would be back when he woke up. Then no one else would have to think or worry, just work and be glad about the day, the grain, and freedom.

But the disagreement lingered in the hall, dividing the thralls into two opposing camps. One group feared the dangerous freedom that the woman had so aptly described. The other group, comprising the strongest men, wanted to fight and live in peace rather than give up. But all of them longed for the massive figure who could calm the waters and guide them with few words and little trouble.

The sun rose from the sea into a clear sky, and they started working the grain early. Men were sharpening their scythes on pieces of slate, sending a ringing, grinding sound out over the shore and lake, and two of them were already out fishing.

The women tied the grain in sheaves and stood them in the field to dry. The grain was rich and heavy, but there was no happiness in the harvest. Uncertainty affected everyone, and they turned toward the forest again and again. The riders might burst out again at any moment and surround them. Some had galloped straight through the field, trampling down the stalks. The harvesters tried to reassure each other that the enemy was far, far away and didn't give a damn about them anyway after capturing Holme and his family. But it didn't help.

Around midday, they saw a man standing at the edge of the forest watching them. He was an older man, who probably meant them no harm, but they were edgy and suspicious. They thought he might be a spy, who would lead the enemy to them, so they threw down their scythes for their axes and spears. The man saw what they did and ran into the forest. The men chased him, whooping and yelling, but soon returned. He had either gotten away or was a forest creature. You saw them every once in a while at abandoned farmsteads. They had seen this one flutter among the thickets and then vanish.

The men laughed raucously about the brief hunt and the mood lightened. They had agreed from the beginning that when the grain was cut and ready here, they'd move on to Holme's settlement and harvest the crop there. Otherwise, someone else might at any minute. During hard times, there were a lot of people—individuals and families—lurking at the forest's edge.

No one mentioned what they were going to do after all the work was finished, but it hung in the air around them. They didn't want to live with this apprehension and uncertainty; they had to know what was going on in town once the riders arrived with their prisoners. Maybe they could be of some help to Holme and the others. At the very least they could find out what dangers to expect from town.

When they peered out from the edge of the forest at the settlement all was peaceful. Everybody—both women and men—had walked there. They felt like a group of fatherless brothers and sisters without Holme. They had seen hoofprints all along the soft forest road and knew that the riders had spent the night at the settlement. Part of the grain had been reaped, and the millstone showed signs of recent use. Either the riders or the forest dwellers might be responsible.

Something was missing from the slope, and it took a while before they realized that the charred god was no longer standing on its rock. The men went searching through the dense brush down below and soon found the blackened clump of wood. The riders had knocked it off its perch but had forgotten—or decided not—to destroy it. The thralls put it back in place, thinking that it would probably take their and Holme's side. They would sacrifice some of their goods to the wooden god before evening.

The next day everything was ready. The grain was drying, and the women could take care of whatever was still left to do by themselves. A couple of the older men would stay behind too. The men still hadn't said anything, but the women looked at them anxiously. They sensed that they were going to be left unprotected, perhaps for good, becoming prey to outlaws and other men from the woods.

The men gathered by the smithy in the cleft, and soon you could hear the clanging and rasping sounds as they repaired and sharpened their weapons. A couple of them sat fixing their shoes in the sunshine on the slope. The women cleaned and ground grain so the men could have bread for the journey, and there was still some fish left from the previous day.

They spent all day in preparation and then retired at dusk. They weren't sure exactly what to do, but they had to do some-thing. Without Holme, the forest no longer felt safe. They had to know what was in store for them. The skeptical woman jeered again at this oppressive thing they called freedom, but grew silent when no one responded.

They rose at first light to be on their way, a curious, silent band who, shivering in the morning cold, gathered outside the building and strapped on their weapons. The grass under their feet felt stiff from the frost but was almost warm at the edge of the forest. As Holme had done many times before, the thralls turned around and looked down over the settlement. They doubtless wondered if this could be the last time they would see it, if they were going off to pay for their year of freedom with their lives.

When the men were completely out of sight, the women with-drew into the building and barred the door. A few of them were cry-ing; others were criticizing the men who had just abandoned them. The two older men who had remained behind were silent; they were aware that the women didn't think they counted for much.

After a while the sun came up, and a pale red glow fell on the buildings and the edge of the forest. A ray of light touched the blackened god and shone on a cooked fish lying on the stone before him. Beside it lay a piece of last night's bread, bran and charcoal baked into it.

From the fortress, the chieftain watched the enemy gathering in the open area, preparing to cast lots. Their behavior and talk told him that a great deal was at stake.

He was able to pick up a few indistinct voices asking the god if this town was theirs to plunder and burn. There was complete silence when the dice fell; then he heard a disappointed howl from a hundred throats. But the chieftain brightened, hoping again for salvation. Surely Christ had heard his plea for help and had directed the roll of the dice.

A few more questions were settled by lot, and then there was a meeting, which ended with most of the warriors withdrawing from the fortress and walking toward the ships. The chieftain yelled out the miracle triumphantly, and a roar of surprise and joy answered him. Christ was still the mightiest of gods. As many people as could find room ran up onto the barricade to see the departing enemy for themselves.

The land's former king stood with his men, the smallest part of the enemy army. The others were hastily tending to their ships; the wind was good and all the other signs favorable for the journey. Their god had promised them another, richer town if they left this one alone. It wasn't long before two-thirds of the ships were on their way, and their rhythmical chants could be heard clear up to the fortress.

But the fortress gates did not open. No one knew what those staying behind had in mind. If they attacked, there was hope of defending the fortress for a while. A message had been sent to the king to come back soon with his men.

A horn blast sounded outside, and the fortress fell completely silent. The former king began talking in a friendly voice, offering them friendship and alliance. He was their countryman and didn't want to destroy their town. That was why he had suggested casting of the lots that had ended so fortunately. The Danish chieftain was at that moment on his way to the town the gods had set aside for him to plunder and burn.

The chieftain in the fortress got up on the barricade and said that they had listened with joy to the king's words about friendship and alliance. As far as he was concerned, the king was a man of his word, but the people inside the fortress were frightened and feared treachery; therefore, they wanted warriors from both camps to meet outside first and start the alliance before their eyes. Then everyone would come out and return to his home.

The king agreed, and soon the warriors came down from the barricade. A moment later the gate was opened, and both groups of warriors met in the field while people swarmed above them, eager to see what would happen. It was just as the king had said; no one raised sword or spear against the resident warriors. The alien fleet was sailing east in front of a good wind and soon would be out of sight.[17]

17. Rimbert offers the following description of the Danish raid: "It happened that a certain Swedish king named Anoundus had been driven from his kingdom, and was in exile amongst the Danes. Desiring to regain what had once been his kingdom, he sought aid of them and promised that if they would follow him they would be able to secure much treasure. He offered them Birka . . . they filled twenty-one ships . . . he had eleven of his own ships . . . It so happened that the king of the town was absent . . . Only Herigar, the prefect of this place, was present with the merchants and people who remained there . . . The king beforementioned commanded them to pay a hundred pounds of silver in order to redeem Birka and obtain peace. They forth-

In their great joy, the people forgot all about the prisoners. Only Geire was on his guard. While the people streamed out of the fortress, buzzing with happiness, he approached the chieftain and reminded him about the prisoners. The chieftain knit his brow in irritation and said that they'd be shut in the fortress until he had time to consider the matter. A heavy guard would be posted there so they couldn't escape. Geire himself was the most reliable; he could take as many men as he wanted and take charge of the prisoners. Having said that, the chieftain walked toward town with the foreign king.

The smiths, the last ones to leave the fortress, promised the prisoners they would be hearing from them. The guards angrily shut the gate behind them and didn't respond to their threats that they had better treat the prisoners well.

---

with sent the amount asked and it was received by the king. The Danes resented this agreement, because it was not in accord with their arrangement and they wanted to make a sudden attack upon them and to pillage and burn the place . . . As they were discussing this and were preparing to destroy the town to which the others had fled [i.e., Sigtuna, north of Birka], their design became known to those in the town . . . [who] exhorted one another to make vows and to offer greater sacrifices to their own gods. [Birka's chieftain] Herigar, the faithful servant of the Lord, was angry with them . . . Meanwhile the king proposed to the Danes that they should enquire by the casting of lots whether it was the will of the gods that this place should be ravaged by them . . . As his words were in accord with their custom they could not refuse to adopt the suggestion . . . and they ascertained that it would be impossible to accomplish their purpose . . . and that [instead] they ought to go to a certain town which was situated at a distance on the borders of the lands belonging to the Slavonians. The Danes then, believing that this order had come to them from heaven, retired from this place and hastened to go by a direct route to that town . . . Moreover the king who had come with the object of plundering the Swedes, made peace with them and restored the money that he had recently received from them. He remained also for some time with them as he wished to become reconciled to their nation" (*Anskar*, chapter 19, pp. 65–68).

The grass was yellow and trampled down in the fortress. Pieces of coal, bread, and other scrap lay on the ground, and some of the heavy chests were still there. Inside the atmosphere was oppressive now that everyone was gone, and the joyous noise of the people grew distant and died away in town. The blue sky was clear, and the wind whispered across the blades of grass on the barricade.

Holme's heart ached for freedom. Stone walls rose above him, stifling him, making it impossible for him to see the woods and the lake. He could hear the whispering birch trees on the ramparts and the splashing of the waves against the rocks below. The smiths had gone, the gate had been barred behind them, and their promise to return seemed empty now. Holme had detected a touch of uncertainty in their voices, so he would have to depend on himself alone.

He had talked with the smiths that morning about freedom for the thralls, but they hadn't understood him. There'd always been thralls and always would be. It was good that he considered thralls people and his equals, but how could he think others would ever do so? Chieftains, merchants, and farmers needed thralls, so there would always be thralls. He said he didn't know much more than they did, and it was true that there were countless thralls. But there was also land and forest as far as the eye could see. And the merchants could work for themselves or hire freemen. He had always known in his heart that freedom belonged to everyone, even if he didn't know how it could be attained.

He noticed that the guards were searching for straps to tie them up again. Their wrists still ached. Ausi looked at him with deepening despair and Tora with surprise. The thrall looked at him too, his eyes seeming to ask whether they shouldn't fight instead of getting tied up again. There were five men, including Geire, against them, and Holme and his friend were unarmed.

But when that gate shut, Holme knew he'd fight. He'd been a prisoner for days, had run behind horses, and had lain bound and scorned, waiting for his chance. He'd waited for the smiths, too, but as usual, he was alone. Not completely—the young man by his side could handle at least one of his opponents, maybe two. He was strong and knew what to do. The forest and freedom were outside beckoning with a magnetic force, and Holme probably wasn't the only one feeling that.

Maybe Geire thought that the prisoners weren't dangerous in their new surroundings, that once they were in town, they had resigned themselves to their fate. And his men hadn't been along hunting the thralls down; all they knew was that the master smith, whom they had seen in town before, was guilty of a major crime and would be sentenced. They approached the thralls, arranging the straps as if they were going to bridle horses. Geire stopped a few steps away to watch everything with a furrowed brow. He was still furious that something always came between Holme's sentence and his death.

Holme knew he couldn't delay. The guards were still standing with the straps in their hands when he charged them. But they weren't the ones he had to get to first; Geire, who was standing beside their weapons, was the most dangerous. He could see the sword sliding out of the sheath at the same instant he got him in his grip. . . .

The prisoners had been subdued and compliant in the fortress, so the chieftain would have let them keep their hands untied; he might not even have thought about the fact that the smiths had cut the straps. But when Geire was alone with them and the guards, he ordered them tied up again. He hadn't thought that they were dangerous once they were inside the fortress, but it was important that they not try to escape. They wouldn't be able to climb up the barricade with their hands tied.

While the guards were getting the straps he was thinking about Ausi. He'd soon have a right to her, and no one could stop him once her husband was dead. After days and nights of captivity, this strange woman was still beautiful and enticing. But she kept her eyes affectionately directed the whole time at the dark, silent man by her side.

If Geire had been wholly on his guard, he might have had a chance. He realized he was being charged and started to draw his sword. But he wasn't able to get it into the air before he felt a pair of hands grab him. These were no ordinary hands; he could feel death in their incredible power. He felt himself rise into the air, saw the sky and the stone walls flash before his eyes, and then everything was dark and quiet.

The astonished guards stood stock-still when they saw what had happened to their leader. They weren't ready for an attack; no one had warned them. When Holme seized Geire, the young thrall was instantly on top of one of the guards, grabbing him by the throat and slamming him to the ground. Pinning him there, he took the guard's own short sword and stabbed him where he lay.

The three other guards fled toward the gate as Holme, unarmed, rushed them. The rage emanating from him made them forget about their weapons, but they didn't have time to open the heavy gate before Holme and the thrall were there. After a brief scuffle, five silent men lay inside the fortress, with two men and three women just as silently looking down at them.

Immediately, the five figures walked cautiously out through the gate facing town. The men had taken the guards' weapons, but Holme wasn't happy about the deaths. They hadn't had any choice, of course, but the hunt for them now would be more intense than ever.

There was still no danger from town; most of the inhabitants had either forgotten about the prisoners or thought that they were in safe custody. The boats were still where they had left them, and the doubled-up warrior was lying in the same spot under the bushes. They couldn't see him, but nothing had been disturbed, and big flies were buzzing around the area or sitting almost pensively on the leaves.

You could see the great, silent happiness in the faces of the young thrall and his woman, and you could hear it in their whispers. Even Holme looked relieved, though he alone understood how dangerous their situation was after what had happened at the fortress. Five men were dead; now the enraged king would order the thralls eradicated once and for all. Warriors would ride to the farmsteads once again, and they wouldn't return empty-handed. Holme and the other four had to be gone long before that.

But for now they were still free and had a good head start. Maybe they'd have time to pick up the others from the islet and then go north through unknown, endless forest. It was their only hope and it made Holme's face pensive and subdued even as the others rejoiced about going home. The young man talked the whole time about the fight. He had helped Holme by killing two of the guards; he was proud of that and happy.

In the early afternoon they came to where the path forked toward the separate farmsteads. They stopped to think a moment, then decided to go to the relatives' farmstead first to see if the others were still on the islet. Holme sensed that the men, once they realized that the riders had taken the prisoners away, wouldn't still be walking around there wondering what to do. There were trees there, and they had axes.

The fork was quiet for a while after they left it, but then the sound of footsteps and voices came down the other path from the settlement and the band of thralls came into view. If anyone from either group had yelled, the other group would have heard him. But they were all quiet, and the thralls went on toward town to see what had happened to Holme and, if possible, to find out what was going to happen to them.

Svein reluctantly followed along when everyone was cleared out of the fortress. He had kept close to the prisoners, staring so much at Tora that, tired and angry, she would occasionally crawl behind her father. Svein had hoped they could take the mother and daughter home with them, but the fortress was closed behind them with the prisoners inside. Still, the thralls couldn't get away; Geire was there with several men to watch them.

The crowd streamed down toward the harbor to look at the foreign ships. But Svein stayed behind. The ships would be there a while; he could see them any time. When everyone had passed by, he turned slowly around and walked across the empty meadow. He looked around frequently, expecting his mother to come running after him any minute, anxiety etched in her gray face. She had to stop that; he'd be full-grown soon and would have to go his own way.

He thought he heard something from the fortress and stopped to listen. But all was quiet, so he kept going. Somewhere inside he was afraid that one of the young warriors would look at Tora even though Geire was there with her. She was his alone, and he wouldn't tolerate anyone else even looking at her. He couldn't control his terror of her father—that he knew—but Holme would be dead soon, and then they'd see, the girl and her mother.

The fortress rose mute and lofty above him, and Svein clambered up outside of the rampart. There were openings in the wooden barrier for shooting arrows against attackers, and he looked through one. He saw a warrior lying by the wall, blood running from his beard; another one lay in the middle of the fortress and three more in different positions by the big gate. None of them moved, and the wind passed through the opening beside him. He crouched quickly down, emitted a hoarse sound, and rolled down the rampart. At the bottom, he got up, looked around in terror for Holme, and then dashed toward town, his head lowered like a bull's.

He saw his mother looking for him among the buildings at the edge of town. Breathlessly he told her of the horror he had witnessed, and she began howling and crying in sorrow and rage. So Holme had taken Geire from her too, and now she was alone with her son who was marked for life. That thrall had taken everything from her, and he always got away.

Oblivious to everything else, she rushed toward the harbor. She ran straight to the chieftain and the foreign king, who were standing by the largest dragon ship, and sobbed out what had happened. She demanded revenge. The people crowded around her, listening in surprise to the raging woman before they understood what she was saying. Then some of them started running toward the fortress; several others followed, and soon half the town was on its way back to see what had happened.

The chieftain ordered the island searched and boats sent out to keep the thralls from fleeing to the mainland. No one noticed that a boat had already glided along into the shadow of the mainland forest and that some people were jumping out of it and running into the woods.

The chieftain's wife watched her brother Geire, eyes shut and beard bloody, rocking back and forth on a bier being carried from the fortress. So the smith had finally defeated him. She had only Svein now, and he was still too young to do battle with the deadliest of thralls. She no longer dared hope that the chieftain and his warriors would put an end to her enemy.

Inside the fortress the chieftain told the thrall smith's story to the foreign king—about his many deeds of violence, his thinking the thralls could be free, and his power. They were surprised that Geire had only a head wound visible, and they could guess what had happened. Blood was running from two of the men, but the other two just seemed to be asleep. The people standing there murmured with fear and reluctant admiration that Holme had crushed them to death with his bare hands.

The foreign king marveled and said that he'd like very much to see such a man. He asked why they hadn't made him a warrior long ago and tried to win his goodwill. It would be worthwhile making a man like that your friend. He had heard and could see what it was like to have him for an enemy.

But the chieftain refused to listen to such talk. No freeman would lower himself to seek the goodwill of a runaway slave, and this was the last straw. The next time they got hold of Holme, he would be cut down on the spot; taking him prisoner was foolhardy. And his fellow thralls would be rooted out to the last man. The smith's dangerous longing for freedom would disappear with them and order would be restored in the land.

Holme and his companions were pleased to see the grain drying and everything in order. The raft was tied at the landing, waves washing over it. The boats hadn't been touched. There was no life at the farmstead, but it wasn't difficult to figure out where the people were. Holme was pleased to think that the thralls could get along without his leadership and help.

They would spend the night here and follow them the next morning. The women were soon busy cleaning the grain, and the men went fishing by the landing. They might have time to clean most of the grain to take along before their enemies caught up with them.

The days were growing shorter, and the darkness would help them escape to the north. They would keep someone constantly on guard at the farmsteads so they wouldn't have to flee until the last minute. Something might delay the pursuit.

The next morning they took the little boat to the settlement. The young thrall and his woman rowed, joking and laughing. Ausi and Holme watched the shore from which they had once fled the settlement—the stones, the reeds, the dark forest that reached all the way down to the water. But even before Holme caught sight of the settlement, he knew something was wrong. It was quiet and deserted; the grain stood drying here, too, but there were no happy voices or other human sounds. It was with great relief that he finally saw one of the older men by the shore.

The women came running to the boat when it pulled up, but their excitement soon turned to despair when they saw that their men hadn't come back with them. Holme listened quietly to their story, fatigue enveloping his face. He had looked forward to a couple of quiet days before the great flight north, but now he had to return to town. If the men got there first, it would be their death because of what had happened. The people's revenge would destroy the first ones to appear. It might already be too late. But they had known it would be dangerous; maybe he could still catch them.

Both the older men wanted to go along, but he refused. Ausi and Tora also wanted to go with him, but he refused them, too. He had traveled between settlement and town many times, but this trip would be the roughest and most dangerous. And before he had understood what freedom was and had had so many people to answer for, he had always managed best by himself. If the enemy came, he would probably be aware of it in plenty of time.

As Holme prepared for the return trip, the women became petulant. They said straight out that things had been better for them before. They hadn't had to live in constant danger then. And why should they get husbands if they were only to be taken away from them? They looked askance at Holme and his family. Ausi snapped back at them, but Holme was quiet, seeming not to hear them. The important thing now was the men who had gone to town. What to do afterward they would decide together—if they were ever together again. Besides, the women were anxious about their husbands; it was best to pay no attention to them.

He told the men what to do while they waited. With the women's help, they should clean as much grain as possible. They might have to break camp quickly when he returned with the other men. But he noticed that even the two older men looked at him differently now that things weren't going so well. Perhaps they missed their slavery, too, and despised freedom when it meant they had to do something for it. They were probably afraid, like Stor and Tan. Those journeying to town, however, had shown that they understood what he had meant by freedom.

The boat was gone by the time he reached the shore opposite the island, and he knew his men were in it. A hermit who lived just inside the forest told him that a lot had been happening in town the last few days. And Holme heard a skewed account about what he had done and about the canceled attack on the town. In answer to his question, the hermit said that some badly dressed men had come down out of the forest and had taken the boat. They had waited for dusk before daring to venture across.

Holme traded some provisions for the hermit's boat, which lay hidden in the reeds. The hermit walked in front of him, whining about what a great burden it would be for him if he didn't get his boat back. He'd starve to death because he subsisted on fish. Without a word, Holme took out the silver he still had left and put it in the hermit's outstretched hand. He skirted the reeds a while before setting course for the wooded side of the island.

A small ship from inside the coves crossed his path and the oarsmen saw him but nothing happened. He had seen the alien vessels in the harbor, but now the mountain blocked them from view. It was a clear autumn day with a cool breeze that intensified the farther out you rowed. He could see horses and people by the ferry in the distance. An occasional shout or other sound wafted across the water.

Holme didn't know how he was going to save his men, but he hoped they were still loose and hiding in the island forests. All he had to do was find them and get back to the farmsteads before their enemies did. Everyone knew where the thralls' hideaway was and would ride right to it.

He scoured the shore and finally saw their boat. It was floating in the reeds, and he tied the hermit's boat beside it and went ashore. He couldn't see or hear anything except some cows ambling around in the forest on the shore, snorting and rustling in the thickets.

Holme began to search but found no trace of his men. After circling round, he happened onto the countless burial mounds. One or two other people were walking around there, visible on a mound for a moment, or disappearing between them. Holme watched them closely without getting any nearer, but they weren't out after him. He decided to walk to the woods on the other side of the graveyard and search there. The wind was whistling across the mounds, and the leaves on a lone aspen tree were dancing and twinkling.

Holme walked out in the open; no one would suspect him of being up here. The woods began where the mounds grew sparser, and many men were moving about there; he could hear spades clanging against stone. He crouched down, crept along a mound, and looked cautiously through the tall blades of grass on the top. The autumn sun was shining brightly, making it difficult to see into the trees.

When Holme finally figured out what was going on, he just stopped, maybe because the activity reflected a kind of peace, the end of a battle. For the first time he felt defeat and despair. Some men were digging in the darkness of the forest, and others lay in a silent, motionless row, waiting for their graves. Holme couldn't recognize them from that distance, but he didn't have to. He knew he had come too late this time.

He could feel, stronger than ever before, the power of the freemen leveled against him. He had no intention of attacking and killing any of the gravediggers; that wouldn't gain him anything. And he remembered the men and women at the settlement, who still needed him.

Holme didn't know how the men had died, but they had probably been taken while the townsfolk were still in a fury over the siege and the killings in the fortress. No one would bother bringing a pack of thralls before the assembly. They would just kill them, and there they lay all in a row. The branches swayed, causing sun and shadow to flicker on their tattered clothes. A few men and women stood in silence to one side. They might have known the dead men, or maybe they had just followed along out of curiosity.

Before the men had finished burying the thralls, Holme had slid down and sneaked away among the mounds. He reached the boat and rowed across as though in a dream. The hermit chattered happily about getting his boat back again, but the hard face neither looked at him nor answered his words. Holme cast a final look at the town before disappearing into the forest.

Two joyous shouts greeted him when he emerged from the forest. His wife and daughter ran to him and told him they were alone. The older men and the rest of the women had taken the large boat and as much grain as they could carry. The younger couple had gone to the other farmstead to harvest as much grain as they could. They probably hoped it would be theirs someday after the pursuit had ended and the danger had passed.

Holme felt somehow relieved. Now he didn't have to tell what he had seen under the spruce trees on the island. No one would bother taking revenge on the two old men and the women, even if it was discovered they had belonged to the free thralls.

But what about themselves? They could stay at the settlement for one night, but no more. They would mill grain all night and take as much as possible with them. Holme could hide the rest in the forest. The cave would be their home, just like the old days.

As at every other great change in his life, Holme lay awake the first night in the cave, thinking everything over. They weren't sleeping on moss as they had before; this time they had animal skins and clothes. Sixteen summers had passed since they hid in the cave with their newborn baby. The coarse pine trees on the gravel ridge were the same, but the pine forest in the marshland had grown taller and denser.

Tora had fallen asleep at once, but Ausi had only recently dozed off. She had insisted on staying awake and coming to him the first night in the cave, remembering all that had happened there. She didn't grieve over what they had just lost, and Holme was grateful to her for that.

He was alone again now with his freedom. Those who had understood it and shared it with him had died for it, but the others hadn't been strong enough to bear the burden. He hoped the dead men had attained freedom in the land they inhabited now. No one else here would know what freedom was after he was gone. Somehow he had to teach others about it while he was still alive. He owed it to those dead men to keep freedom alive.

Holme thought a moment about the provisions those men would need on their journey to the other land. He could have dug them up and put the provisions in. They had their weapons; he had seen them lying beside their owners, waiting. No one would rob even his enemy of weapons on the unknown journey.

Holme missed nothing he had lost, not the smithy in town, not the house, not the settlement they had just left. The safest hiding place they could find was here; the forest whispered outside the cave, they had grain, and he could get meat with his weapons. There was water in the spring below. But he wouldn't be able to stay in the forest and live out his life. He had the burden of freedom to carry, and he had to go out with it to the countless thralls who were suffering pain, who were being whipped and killed whenever it pleased their masters. He must try to explain freedom to them; then they could do as they pleased.

The last time had been hard, and he felt depleted. His wife and daughter lay sleeping beside him, and he hoped he could stay alive to protect them. He was the only one; neither Christ nor the wooden gods could or would. He'd had enough proof of that.

In town he had longed for the whistling of the forest; now it was coming to him again. As he listened, he immediately felt how insignificant what happened outside the forest was. It was pleasant to sleep in the whispering woods; maybe they could tell him how to help his fellow thralls gain their freedom.

Ausi woke up at dawn and saw the jagged rock hanging just above her face. She smiled with a sense of well-being when she remembered where she was. They were together. They had grain and water; Christ and Holme would take care of the rest. It was too bad about the men who had been killed in town, but the most important thing was that Holme was still alive. Anybody could see now that Christ walked with and protected Holme. Christ Himself had been beaten and persecuted; that was why He was on the side of Holme and the thralls. And He had doubtlessly taken charge of the dead thralls and given them freedom and everything they wanted in heaven.

Ausi was back in her first home, and it felt good, although Holme would have to make some changes before winter. Their enemies might be searching for them in the forest that very day, but that didn't bother her. There was One standing by their side protecting them. And if they were captured, she and Tora would follow Holme in death. They must be together on the last journey so she could explain everything to Christ. No, as far as she could see, there was nothing to fear.

They were like a dream, those sixteen years since she had lain there with her newborn, Tora, with Holme standing naked outside the cave. It smelled of earth and moss as it had then, and the forest whispered now too. When Holme and Tora woke up, it would be nice to talk about the future.

She felt great affection for her husband and daughter and gently caressed them. She could hear the morning caw of the crows outside and imagined them flying over the marshy ground, searching for food.

But in town the same morning, a powerful division of warriors was being outfitted to capture and kill the man who dared say that freedom belonged to all mankind.

Selected Bibliography

Translations

Fridegård, Jan. *I, Lars Hård (Jag Lars Hård,* 1935). Translated and with an introduction and notes by Robert E. Bjork. Lincoln and London: University of Nebraska Press, 1983.

—. Jacob's Ladder (*Tack för himlastegen,* 1936) and *Mercy (Barmhärtighet,* 1936). Translated and with introductions and notes by Robert E. Bjork. Lincoln and London: University of Nebraska Press, 1985.

—. "The Key" ("Nyckeln," 1944). Translated by Robert E. Bjork. *Translation: The Journal of Literary Translation* 15 (1985): 270–75.

—. *Land of Wooden Gods (Trägudars land,* 1940). Translated and with an afterword and notes by Robert E. Bjork. Lincoln and London: University of Nebraska Press, 1989.

———. "Natural Selection" ("Det naturliga urvalet," 1939). Translated by Robert E. Bjork. *Malahat Review* 55 (1980): 104–10.

———. "1987 Translation Prize Selection from *Land of Wooden Gods.*" Translated by Robert E. Bjork. *Scandinavian Review* 76, no. 4 (1988): 77–82.

———. "100 Kilos Rye" ("Kvarnbudet," 1944). Translated by Robert E. Bjork. *Scandinavian Review* 68, no. 2 (1980): 54–62.

Criticism

Gamby, Erik. *Jan Fridegård. Introduktion till ett författarskap.* Stockholm: Svenska bokförlaget, 1956.

Graves, Peter. *Jan Fridegård: Lars Hård.* Studies in Swedish Literature, no. 8. Hull: University of Hull, 1977. (In English.)

Lundkvist, Artur and Lars Forssell, eds. *Jan Fridegård.* Stockholm: Förlaget frilansen, 1949.

Schön, Ebbe. *Jan Fridegård och forntiden. En studie i diktverk och källor.* Uppsala, Sweden: Almqvist & Wiksell, 1973.

———. *Jan Fridegård. Proletärdiktaren och folkkulturen.* Stockholm: Wahlström & Widstrand, 1978.